Anxiety and Panic Attacks

ANXIETY AND PANIC ATTACKS

Your Questions Answered

Daniel Zwillenberg

Q&A Health Guides

GREENWOOD™

An Imprint of ABC-CLIO, LLC

Santa Barbara, California • Denver, Colorado

Library of Congress Cataloging-in-Publication Data

Names: Zwillenberg, Daniel, author.
Title: Anxiety and panic attacks : your questions answered / Daniel Zwillenberg.
Description: Santa Barbara, California : Greenwood, an imprint of ABC-CLIO, LLC,
    [2018] | Series: Q&A health guides | Includes bibliographical references and index.
Identifiers: LCCN 2017058623 (print) | LCCN 2017059588 (ebook) |
    ISBN 9781440852992 (ebook) | ISBN 9781440852985 (print : alk. paper)
Subjects: LCSH: Panic attacks—Popular works. | Anxiety disorders—Popular works.
Classification: LCC RC535 (ebook) | LCC RC535 .Z85 2018 (print) |
    DDC 616.85/223—dc23
LC record available at https://lccn.loc.gov/2017058623

ISBN: 978-1-4408-5298-5 (print)
      978-1-4408-5299-2 (ebook)

22 21 20 19 18   1 2 3 4 5

This book is also available as an eBook.

Greenwood
An Imprint of ABC-CLIO, LLC

ABC-CLIO, LLC
130 Cremona Drive, P.O. Box 1911
Santa Barbara, California 93116-1911
www.abc-clio.com

This book is printed on acid-free paper ∞

Manufactured in the United States of America

Contents

Series Foreword

All of us have questions about our health. Is this normal? Should I be doing something differently? Whom should I talk to about my concerns? And our modern world is full of answers. Thanks to the Internet, there's a wealth of information at our fingertips, from forums where people can share their personal experiences to Wikipedia articles to the full text of medical studies. But finding the right information can be an intimidating and difficult task—some sources are written at too high a level, others have been oversimplified, while still others are heavily biased or simply inaccurate.

Q&A Health Guides address the needs of readers who want accurate, concise answers to their health questions, authored by reputable and objective experts, and written in clear and easy-to-understand language. This series focuses on the topics that matter most to young adult readers, including various aspects of physical and emotional well-being as well as other components of a healthy lifestyle. These guides will also serve as a valuable tool for parents, school counselors, and others who may need to answer teens' health questions.

All books in the series follow the same format to make finding information quick and easy. Each volume begins with an essay on health literacy and why it is so important when it comes to gathering and evaluating health information. Next, the top five myths and misconceptions that surround the topic are dispelled. The heart of each guide is a collection of questions and answers, organized thematically. A selection of five case studies provides real-world examples to illuminate key concepts. Rounding out each volume is a directory of resources, glossary, and index.

It is our hope that the books in this series will not only provide valuable information but will also help guide readers toward a lifetime of healthy decision making.

Acknowledgments

I would like to thank Maxine Taylor for her guidance throughout this process, and my friend, colleague, and mentor, Blaise Aguirre, for suggesting that I write this book. I would also like to thank everyone who read incomplete drafts and shared their honest feedback, including my father, David Zwillenberg, and mother-in-law, Lisa Schreiber.

I feel fortunate to have earned my doctorate at Yeshiva University's Ferkauf Graduate School of Psychology, where I had the privilege of being trained in a program directed by Dr. Abe Givner. I am grateful to the many supervisors—particularly Drs. Alec Miller and Lata McGinn—who offered me the benefit of their expertise, as well as to my colleagues at McLean Hospital's 3East DBT Program.

I would like to express my gratitude to the many clients who have shared with me their pain and joy and have entrusted me with their most private selves.

Most importantly, I would like to express my deepest love and appreciation to my wife, Karen, who allowed me to dedicate a truly excessive amount of time to this project. I also want to thank my children, Jacob, Noah, and Emily, whose patience (and relatively good behavior) afforded me the opportunity to work on this book. To my siblings, I would like to point out that I wrote a book and you didn't. Just an observation.

Introduction

Anxiety and fear are normal features of the human experience. These emotions are described in some of humanity's earliest written records, and they appear to exist across all known cultures. When anxiety and fear happen in the appropriate context and at an intensity that matches the situation, they help people escape danger or cope with an anticipated challenge. When anxiety and fear happen in the wrong context or at an inappropriately high intensity, they are no longer helpful. When this occurs repeatedly, anxiety and fear can lead to distress and dysfunction, resulting in an anxiety disorder.

Anxiety disorders, which have only existed as a widely recognized diagnostic category since 1980, are remarkably common. As a group, anxiety disorders are the most prevalent mental health conditions in the United States and across the world. According to the National Institutes of Mental Health (NIMH), 18.1 percent of American adults—40 million people—have had an anxiety disorder over the previous 12 months. NIMH estimates that 28.8 percent of U.S. adults have an anxiety disorder at some point in their lifetimes. Most anxiety disorders start in childhood or adolescence, and when untreated, they can last for many years. Anxiety disorders generate emotional suffering and lower quality of life, and cause impairments in work, school, and social relationships.

Research on anxiety disorders has come a long way in a brief span of time. Just a few hundred years ago, there was widespread agreement that mental illness was caused by sin or demonic possession. Today, scientists are generating a steady stream of insights into the brain structures, neurotransmitters, and thought processes that are associated with fear and anxiety, as well as the genetic and environmental factors that influence the development of anxiety disorders. In 1927, there were only three papers published on the topic of anxiety in academic journals; today, thousands are published annually. A little over 100 years ago, patients with symptoms of anxiety were commonly diagnosed with the catch-all label of "neurasthenia," which had little scientific basis and even less therapeutic value. Today, investigators are applying advanced statistical methods to identify subtypes of anxiety disorders and are using these data to develop more effective treatments.

This book represents an attempt to distill some of the fundamental concepts from the diverse body of anxiety research and to answer the questions that I have heard most frequently from my clients or wondered about myself. By necessity, I have had to omit a great deal of information, but I have tried to include those ideas and theories that are most relevant to the field of psychology in general and to anxiety research in particular.

Guide to Health Literacy

On her 13th birthday, Samantha was diagnosed with type 2 diabetes. She consulted her mom and her aunt, both of whom also have type 2 diabetes, and decided to go with their strategy of managing diabetes by taking insulin. As a result of participating in an after-school program at her middle school that focused on health literacy, she learned that she can help manage the level of glucose in her bloodstream by counting her carbohydrate intake, following a diabetic diet, and exercising regularly. But, what exactly should she do? How does she keep track of her carbohydrate intake? What is a diabetic diet? How long should she exercise and what type of exercise should she do? Samantha is a visual learner, so she turned to her favorite source of media, YouTube, to answer these questions. She found videos from individuals around the world sharing their experiences and tips, doctors (or at least people who have "Dr." in their YouTube channel names), government agencies such as the National Institutes of Health, and even video clips from cat lovers who have cats with diabetes. With guidance from the librarian and the health and science teachers at her school, she assessed the credibility of the information in these videos and even compared their suggestions to some of the print resources that she was able to find at her school library. Now, she knows exactly how to count her carbohydrate level, how to prepare and follow a diabetic diet, and how much (and what) exercise is needed daily. She intends to share her findings with her mom and her aunt, and now she wants to create a chart that summarizes what she has learned that she can share with her doctor.

Samantha's experience is not unique. She represents a shift in our society; an individual no longer views himself or herself as a passive recipient of medical care but as an active mediator of his or her own health. However, in this era when any individual can post his or her opinions and experiences with a particular health condition online with just a few clicks or publish a memoir, it is vital that people know how to assess the credibility of health information. Gone are the days when "publishing" health information required intense vetting. The health information landscape is highly saturated, and people have innumerable sources where they can find information about practically any health topic. The sources (whether print, online, or a person) that an individual consults for health information are crucial because the accuracy and trustworthiness of the information can potentially affect his or her overall health. The ability to find, select, assess, and use health information constitutes a type of literacy—health literacy—that everyone must possess.

THE DEFINITION AND PHASES OF HEALTH LITERACY

One of the most popular definitions for health literacy comes from Ratzan and Parker (2000), who describe health literacy as "the degree to which individuals have the capacity to obtain, process, and understand basic health information and services needed to make appropriate health decisions." Recent research has extrapolated health literacy into health literacy bits, further shedding light on the multiple phases and literacy practices that are embedded within the multifaceted concept of health literacy. Although this research has focused primarily on online health information seeking, these health literacy bits are needed to successfully navigate both print and online sources. There are six phases of health information seeking: (1) Information Need Identification and Question Formulation, (2) Information Search, (3) Information Comprehension, (4) Information Assessment, (5) Information Management, and (6) Information Use.

The first phase is the *information need identification and question formulation phase*. In this phase, one needs to be able to develop and refine a range of questions to frame one's search and understand relevant health terms. In the second phase, *information search*, one has to possess appropriate searching skills, such as using proper keywords and correct spelling in search terms, especially when using search engines and databases.

It is also crucial to understand how search engines work (i.e., how search results are derived, what the order of the search results means, how to use the snippets that are provided in the search results list to select websites, and how to determine which listings are ads on a search engine results page). One also has to limit reliance on surface characteristics, such as the design of a website or a book (a website or book that appears to have a lot of information or looks aesthetically pleasant does not necessarily mean it has good information) and language used (a website or book that utilizes jargon, the keywords that one used to conduct the search, or the word "information" does not necessarily indicate it will have good information). The next phase is *information comprehension*, whereby one needs to have the ability to read, comprehend, and recall the information (including textual, numerical, and visual content) one has located from the books and/or online resources.

To assess the credibility of health information (*information assessment* phase), one needs to be able to evaluate information for accuracy, evaluate how current the information is (e.g., when a website was last updated or when a book was published), and evaluate the creators of the source—for example, examine site sponsors or type of sites (.com, .gov, .edu, or .org) or the author of a book (practicing doctor, a celebrity doctor, a patient of a specific disease, etc.) to determine the believability of the person/ organization providing the information. Such credibility perceptions tend to become generalized, so they must be frequently reexamined (e.g., the belief that a specific news agency always has credible health information needs continuous vetting). One also needs to evaluate the credibility of the medium (e.g., television, Internet, radio, social media, and book) and evaluate—not just accept without questioning—others' claims regarding the validity of a site, book, or other specific source of information. At this stage, one has to "make sense of information gathered from diverse sources by identifying misconceptions, main and supporting ideas, con-flicting information, point of view, and biases" (American Association of School Librarians [AASL], 2009, p. 13) and conclude which sources/ information are valid and accurate by using conscious strategies rather than simply using intuitive judgments or "rules of thumb." This phase is the most challenging segment of health information seeking and serves as a determinant of success (or lack thereof) in the information-seeking process. The following section on Sources of Health Information further explains this phase.

The fifth phase is *information management*, whereby one has to orga-nize information that has been gathered in some manner to ensure easy retrieval and use in the future. The last phase is *information use*, in which one will synthesize information found across various resources, draw conclusions, and locate the answer to his or her original question and/or the content that fulfills the information need. This phase also often involves implementation, such as using the information to solve a health problem; make health-related decisions; identify and engage in behaviors that will help a person to avoid health risks; share the health information found with family members and friends who may benefit from it; and advocate more broadly for personal, family, or community health.

THE IMPORTANCE OF HEALTH LITERACY

The conception of health has moved from a passive view (someone is either well or ill) to one that is more active and process based (someone is working toward preventing or managing disease). Hence, the dominant focus has shifted from doctors and treatments to patients and prevention, resulting in the need to strengthen our ability and confidence (as patients and consumers of health care) to look for, assess, understand, manage, share, adapt, and use health-related information. An individual's health literacy level has been found to predict his or her health status better than age, race, educational attainment, employment status, and income level (National Network of Libraries of Medicine, 2013). Greater health literacy also enables individuals to better communicate with health care providers such as doctors, nutritionists, and therapists, as they can pose more relevant, informed, and useful questions to health care providers. Another added advantage of greater health literacy is better information-seeking skills, not only for health but also in other domains, such as completing assignments for school.

SOURCES OF HEALTH INFORMATION: THE GOOD, THE BAD, AND THE IN-BETWEEN

For generations, doctors, nurses, nutritionists, health coaches, and other health professionals have been the trusted sources of health information. Additionally, researchers have found that young adults, when they have health-related questions, typically turn to a family member who has had firsthand experience with a health condition because of their family member's close proximity and because of their past experience with, and trust in, this individual. Expertise should be a core consideration when consulting a person, website, or book for health information. The credentials and background of the person or author and conflicting interests of the author (and his or her organization) must be checked and validated to ensure the likely credibility of the health information they are conveying. While books often have implied credibility because of the peer-review process involved, self-publishing has challenged this credibility, so qualifications of book authors should also be verified. When it comes to health information, currency of the source must also be examined. When examining health information/studies presented, pay attention to the exhaustiveness of research methods utilized to offer recommendations or conclusions. Small and nondiverse sample size is often—but not always—an indication of reduced credibility. Studies that confuse correlation with causation is another potential issue to watch for. Information seekers must also pay attention to the sponsors of the research studies. For example, if a study is sponsored by manufacturers of drug Y and the study recommends that drug Y is the best treatment to manage or cure a disease, this may indicate a lack of objectivity on the part of the researchers.

The Internet is rapidly becoming one of the main sources of health information. Online forums, news agencies, personal blogs, social media sites, pharmacy sites, and celebrity "doctors" are all offering medical and health information targeted to various types of people in regard to all types of diseases and symptoms. There are professional journalists, citizen journalists, hoaxers, and people paid to write fake health news on various sites that may appear to have a legitimate domain name and may even have authors who claim to have professional credentials, such as an MD. All these sites *may* offer useful information or information that appears to be useful and relevant; however, much of the information may be debatable and may fall into gray areas that require readers to discern credibility, reliability, and biases.

While broad recognition and acceptance of certain media, institutions, and people often serve as the most popular determining factors to assess credibility of health information among young people, keep in mind that there are legitimate Internet sites, databases, and books that publish health information and serve as sources of health information for doctors, other health sites, and members of the public. For example, MedlinePlus (https://medlineplus.gov) has trusted sources on over 975 diseases and conditions and presents the information in easy-to-understand language.

The chart here presents factors to consider when assessing credibility of health information. However, keep in mind that these factors function only as a guide and require continuous updating to keep abreast with the changes in the landscape of health information, information sources, and technologies.

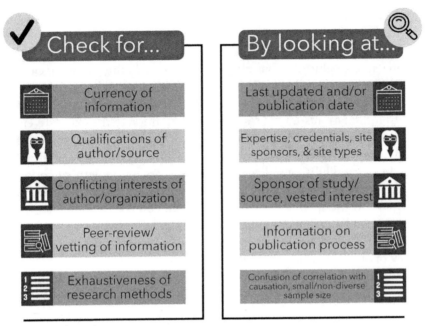

All images from flaticon.com

The chart can serve as a guide; however, approaching a librarian about how one can go about assessing the credibility of both print and online health information is far more effective than using generic checklist-type tools. While librarians are not health experts, they can apply and teach patrons strategies to determine the credibility of health information.

With the prevalence of fake sites and fake resources that appear to be legitimate, it is important to use the following health information assessment tips to verify health information that one has obtained (St. Jean et al., 2015, p. 151):

- **Don't assume you are right**: Even when you feel very sure about an answer, keep in mind that the answer may not be correct, and it is important to conduct (further) searches to validate the information.
- **Don't assume you are wrong**: You may actually have correct information, even if the information you encounter does not match—that is, you may be right and the resources that you have found may contain false information.
- **Take an open approach**: Maintain a critical stance by not including your preexisting beliefs as keywords (or letting them influence your choice of keywords) in a search, as this may influence what it is possible to find out.

- **Verify, verify, and verify**: Information found, especially on the Internet, needs to be validated, no matter how the information appears on the site (i.e., regardless of the appearance of the site or the quantity of information that is included).

Health literacy comes with experience navigating health information. Professional sources of health information, such as doctors, health care providers, and health databases, are still the best, but one also has the power to search for health information and then verify it by consulting with these trusted sources and by using the health information assessment tips and guide shared previously.

Mega Subramaniam, PhD
Associate Professor, College of Information Studies,
University of Maryland

REFERENCES AND FURTHER READING

American Association of School Librarians (AASL). (2009). *Standards for the 21st-century learner in action.* Chicago, IL: American Association of School Librarians.

Hilligoss, B., & Rieh, S.-Y. (2008). Developing a unifying framework of credibility assessment: Construct, heuristics, and interaction in context. *Information Processing & Management, 44*(4), 1467–1484.

Kuhlthau, C. C. (1988). Developing a model of the library search process: Cognitive and affective aspects. *Reference Quarterly, 28*(2), 232–242.

National Network of Libraries of Medicine (NNLM). (2013). Health literacy. Bethesda, MD: National Network of Libraries of Medicine. Retrieved from nnlm.gov/outreach/consumer/hlthlit.html

Ratzan, S. C., & Parker, R. M. (2000). Introduction. In C. R. Selden, M. Zorn, S. C. Ratzan, & R. M. Parker (Eds.), *National Library of Medicine current bibliographies in medicine: Health literacy.* NLM Pub. No. CBM 2000-1. Bethesda, MD: National Institutes of Health, U.S. Department of Health and Human Services.

St. Jean, B., Subramaniam, M., Taylor, N. G., Follman, R., Kodama, C., & Casciotti, D. (2015). The influence of positive hypothesis testing on youths' online health-related information seeking. *New Library World, 116*(3/4), 136–154.

St. Jean, B., Taylor, N. G., Kodama, C., & Subramaniam, M. (2017, February). Assessing the health information source perceptions of tweens using card-sorting exercises. *Journal of Information Science*. Retrieved from http://journals.sagepub.com/doi/abs/10.1177/0165551516687728

Subramaniam, M., St. Jean, B., Taylor, N. G., Kodama, C., Follman, R., & Casciotti, D. (2015). Bit by bit: Using design-based research to improve the health literacy of adolescents. *JMIR Research Protocols*, 4(2), paper e62. Retrieved from http://www.ncbi.nlm.nih.gov/pmc/articles/PMC4464334/

Valenza, J. (2016, November 26). Truth, truthiness, and triangulation: A news literacy toolkit for a "post-truth" world [Web log]. Retrieved from http://blogs.slj.com/neverendingsearch/2016/11/26/truth-truthiness-triangulation-and-the-librarian-way-a-news-literacy-toolkit-for-a-post-truth-world/

---◆◆◆---

Common Myths and Misconceptions about Anxiety and Panic Attacks

1. ANXIETY DISORDERS ARE RARE

Far from being rare, anxiety disorders are the most pervasive category of mental illness in the United States and across the world. According to the National Institutes of Mental Health (NIMH), almost 30 percent of all adults in the United States have had an anxiety disorder at some point in their lives (though far fewer have been diagnosed or treated by a professional). Based on these statistics, it is almost certain that any person living in the United States either suffers from an anxiety disorder or knows someone who suffers from an anxiety disorder. (See Question 9 titled "How common are anxiety disorders? Who tends to get them?" to learn more about the prevalence of anxiety disorders.)

2. PEOPLE DEVELOP ANXIETY DISORDERS BECAUSE OF A TRAUMATIC EVENT/HAVING A BAD CHILDHOOD/POOR GENETICS/ETC.

Researchers have identified several factors that make it more likely that someone will develop an anxiety disorder, meaning that no single cause can explain why any particular individual develops a problem with anxiety while another does not. Though researchers have discovered a variety of biological factors, including genetics, temperament, and gender, as well as environmental factors, which include parental behaviors, traumatic events, and culture, none of these factors in isolation can perfectly predict who will develop an anxiety disorder. (See Question 11 titled "Why do some people develop anxiety disorders?" to learn more about the causes of anxiety disorders.)

3. EVERYONE GETS ANXIOUS, SO ANXIETY DISORDERS ARE NO BIG DEAL, AND PEOPLE SHOULD JUST GET OVER IT

This statement makes as much sense as saying "everyone gets out of breath sometimes, so people with asthma should just breathe better and quit having asthma attacks." Anxiety is a universal human emotion. By definition, however, an anxiety disorder is different from the typical worries, fears, and stresses that people commonly encounter in daily life. People may be diagnosed with an anxiety disorder only if they experience significant distress that is disproportionate to the situation and when their distress impairs their ability to engage with the world around them. Someone with an anxiety disorder cannot simply "get over it" any more than a person can stop an asthma attack through sheer force of will. (See Question 15 titled "When does normal anxiety become a disorder?" to learn more about the difference between normal and pathological anxiety.)

4. THERAPY FOR ANXIETY TAKES YEARS TO WORK

Most people who receive appropriate treatment for anxiety disorders will see a significant improvement over the course of weeks or months—not years. The rate at which people improve depends largely on their willingness to participate in treatment, goodness-of-fit with their therapists, and the duration and severity of their problems. Research has also shown that some anxiety disorders are more readily responsive to medications and therapy than others. For example, phobias have been treated successfully in a single, three-hour session of cognitive-behavioral therapy. (See questions in the "Treatment" section to learn more about the use of medications and pyshcotherapy for anxiety disorders.)

5. PEOPLE WITH ANXIETY DISORDERS SHOULD AVOID STRESSFUL SITUATIONS

While avoiding stressful situations can help people feel better in the short term, avoidance is likely to make anxiety snowball if it becomes habitual.

Avoidance prevents people from learning that a feared situation, such as public speaking, is not truly dangerous, and it also forces people to miss out on many experiences that they might enjoy. People may find that once they start avoiding a situation, their anxiety can take on a life of its own. Avoidance can harden into a vicious cycle, in which distress leads to avoidance, which reinforces anxiety-related thoughts (e.g., "I can't handle my anxiety"). These thoughts, in turn, strengthen the belief that the anxiety-provoking situation is as dangerous as it feels. Avoidance can contribute to the development of an anxiety disorder if people come to rely on it as their primary strategy for managing emotions. (See Question 27 titled "Is it best for people to avoid the things that make them anxious?" to learn more about the impact of avoidance.)

QUESTIONS AND ANSWERS

❖

General Information

1. What is anxiety?

Anxiety appears to be a universal human experience. The emotion exists in all cultures that have been studied and is evident in writings dating back thousands of years. Though some people experience anxiety more frequently and more acutely, it is safe to assume that anyone reading this book will be familiar with what it means to feel anxious. This creates a strange paradox: we all know what anxiety is, but the word has proven itself challenging to define. It is difficult to blame anyone for being confused. The fields of psychology and psychiatry have struggled to define the word "anxiety," even though it is among the most fundamental terms in either discipline.

This problem is due, in part, to the vast number of words that are available to an English speaker to describe the many varieties of fear-based emotional states. People might say that they feel "nervous," "scared," "afraid," "overwhelmed," "apprehensive," "anxious," "on edge," "stressed out," "panicked," "restless," "dread," "alarmed," or "worried." Sometimes, the same word can describe seemingly opposite experiences. People might say that they are "anxious to go to the prom," meaning that they are excited to attend the event, but someone saying "I'm anxious about the prom" is communicating the opposite sentiment. Finding a precise definition of anxiety becomes even more difficult when one considers the way in which laypeople use terms that have a different meaning among professionals.

In the course of a typical day, people may be overheard saying that they "are so OCD" because they like to keep their rooms clean, that their dog gets "anxious" when it hears thunder, or that they are having a "panic attack" because they just learned that they did poorly on an exam.

As pointed out by David Barlow, one of the world's foremost experts on anxiety, the term "anxiety" has been used to describe several emotional states, such as boredom, doubt, and feelings of unreality. Anxiety has also been invoked to describe cognitive problems, such as difficulties with concentration. To complicate matters further, some psychological theories use the term "anxiety" in ways that other theories completely reject. For example, some approaches assume the existence of "unconscious anxiety," while others would argue that this is an oxymoron because anxiety and indeed all emotions are—by definition—conscious experiences.

Anxiety has been conceptualized in so many ways that it is hard to find a single definition that encompasses all of the ways that the term is used, so it is helpful to approach the issue by asking smaller questions.

WHAT IS AN EMOTION?

Most theorists agree that emotions are experienced when an individual perceives a stimulus, which then triggers a physical response (e.g., increased heart rate or change in facial expression). Current theories also recognize that unlike reflexes, which do not require any cognitive evaluation to "fire," emotions involve some form of mental processing. Emotional responses will, therefore, differ based on the individual's life history and the context in which the event occurs. There is also consensus that unlike moods, which do not need to be caused by any specific stimulus and can last hours or days, emotions tend to be relatively short-lived (i.e., seconds or minutes) and are generated by a specific external or internal stimulus.

One of the most influential theories of emotion was advanced in 1872 when Charles Darwin (1809–1882) published *The Expression of the Emotions in Man and Animals*. In this book, Darwin argued that emotions had been preserved by evolution because they helped organisms to survive and pass on their genes to subsequent generations. Pointing to evidence that emotions were displayed with similar facial expressions across cultures around the world, that people who were blind from birth showed the same facial expressions as those with sight, and that nonhuman primates display similar facial responses to those observed in humans, Darwin suggested that emotions are innate or "hardwired."

Proponents of the evolutionary theory of emotions argue that modern human emotions are largely the same as those of early hominids, in whom emotions developed as responses to dangers that existed in their environment. Fear of the dark would have motivated our ancestors to avoid situations that made them vulnerable to being killed by an unseen predator or human rival. Sexual jealousy evolved because it would have reduced sexual infidelity by a partner, whereas sexual desire would have led to increased motivation for mating behavior. Disgust evolved to prevent our ancestors from coming into physical contact with things that caused illness. Compassion and love may have been conserved by evolution because they improved the odds that an individual would protect its offspring or other members of the group.

Subsequent theorists tended to accept the evolutionary basis for emotions but disagreed about whether specific emotions are learned versus innate, and disagreed about the relationship between cognition (i.e., thoughts) and emotion. Noncognitive approaches, such as the James-Lange theory, argued that conscious thought is the result of emotion and not the cause. The neuroscientist Joseph LeDoux (1949–) summarizes James-Lange as stating that contrary to our intuition, we do not run from a bear because we are afraid but rather that "we are afraid because we run." Cognitive theories, such as Schachter and Singer's "two-factor theory" and Richard Lazarus's "appraisal theory," argue instead that an individual's emotional reaction is based on his or her cognitive interpretation of the situation.

Beginning in the 1990s and continuing to today, there has been a growing emphasis on integrating aspects of previous theories. So-called integrationist theories recognize that no single approach, whether based on biology, behavior, or cognition, is sufficient to explain emotion totally, but rather that an accurate account of emotions must involve aspects of all of these systems.

One of these integrative approaches has been proposed by Joseph LeDoux, who argues that evolution has provided mammals with a set of brain circuits that control functions that are important for survival, such as procreation, nutrition, regulation of body temperature, and defense. When one of these survival circuits is activated (e.g., the animal detects that it is dehydrated), the animal is mobilized to find water, and other circuits are inhibited (e.g., the animal will ignore opportunities for sex if its thirst becomes severe enough to threaten its survival). LeDoux argues that in humans, emotions happen when an individual becomes consciously aware of the coordinated effort going on inside his or her brain. The specific emotion that is felt depends on the individual's previous experiences, which determine which label the person selects to describe his or her internal state. (See Question 3 titled "How is the experience of fear 'made' by the brain?" for more information on this theory.)

ANXIETY VERSUS FEAR

Anxiety and fear are so closely intertwined that the terms are often used interchangeably. As components of the body's natural alarm system, these emotions are triggered by signals of danger or threat. Anxiety and fear lead are accompanied by elevated physiological arousal (e.g., increased heart rate and muscular tension). Due to the discomfort that can result from this arousal, people are often motivated to escape or avoid situations that elicit these emotions.

Despite their similarities, there are also meaningful differences between fear and anxiety. Whereas fear is focused on a specific threat that is currently present (e.g., a snarling dog), anxiety is more future-oriented and involves a threat that is vague or unlikely to occur. In some cases, people may experience anxiety without being able to describe what they are anxious "about," but such a nonspecific experience would not fall under the definition of fear. Fear also tends to come on quickly when specific cues are present and dissipates rapidly when the cues are removed. Anxiety, on the other hand, can have a more gradual onset, may not have an identifiable cause, and may last well beyond the end of whatever experience triggered it. Furthermore, in fear, the connection between the emotion and the threat tends to be reasonable, whereas in anxiety, there may be less of a rational relationship between the anxiety-provoking stimulus and the response it evokes. Researchers have also found that different brain structures underlie fear and anxiety.

Although anxiety and fear are quite different on paper, they can be difficult to differentiate in our daily lives. When we feel fear, we almost always evaluate the threat and imagine what its future consequences will be, which would be considered anxiety. Anxiety is also likely to lead to fear, as anxiety makes us more vigilant to danger and therefore more likely to notice stimuli that trigger fear. As an example, if we have just seen a news report about a terrorist attack, this may trigger anxiety-related thoughts about whether we might be attacked in the future. Such thoughts would make us more likely to experience fear if we see something in our environment that signals terrorism-related danger, such as an unaccompanied package on a subway platform.

HELPFUL OR HARMFUL?

Anxiety is a normal human experience, and though it feels unpleasant, it can help people stay vigilant to danger and can motivate them to plan for potential threats. However, anxiety is also implicated in a wide range of psychiatric disorders. Indeed, anxiety disorders are the most common mental illnesses in the United States and across the world. The presence of chronic anxiety contributes to the development of physical illnesses, such as irritable bowel syndrome (IBS) and cardiovascular problems, and also weakens the immune system, which makes people more vulnerable to a variety of medical conditions. High levels of anxiety can lead to dysfunction at school, work, and social relationships. When chronic, anxiety can drive people to depression, substance abuse, and suicide. The determination of whether anxiety has tipped from the side of being reasonable and helpful to the side of being pathological and harmful is based on whether the intensity, frequency, and severity of the anxiety are appropriate to the context in which the anxiety is experienced. (See Question 15 titled "When does normal anxiety become a disorder?" for more information on the line between normal and pathological anxiety.)

SITUATIONAL OR GENERAL?

Anxiety can describe a "state" or a "trait." State anxiety happens only in specific situations, is elicited by particular stimuli, and is short-lived. A fear of dogs, when it occurs in an otherwise calm individual, is an example of state anxiety because it happens in response to a specific stimulus. Trait anxiety refers to a more general, stable aspect of personality, in which an individual experiences the persistent buzzing of anxiety even when he or she cannot identify its external source. The trait of shyness, for example, describes an inhibited style of social interaction that is fairly stable across situations and time. Anxious traits are not necessarily problematic, but the presence of trait anxiety does increase an individual's risk of developing an anxiety disorder.

CONSCIOUS OR UNCONSCIOUS?

Anxiety is a complex phenomenon that involves conscious and unconscious processes. Some experts, such as Joseph LeDoux, argue that anxiety and fear are conscious experiences that are assembled by the brain from nonconscious "ingredients." From this perspective, there is no such thing as unconscious fear or anxiety, because the experience of an emotion—by definition—requires consciousness of a feeling state. In support of this description, research shows that when people are presented with violent images, their heart rates increase, even when the images appear so briefly that subjects are unaware of having seen an image at all. Because they could not consciously apprehend what they had seen, subjects would not have known what had triggered their physiological responses and therefore would not have labeled their emotional experience as anxiety or fear.

For LeDoux, emotions must be consciously experienced, and he suggests that using physiological arousal or escape behaviors as evidence of an emotion only generates confusion and makes it harder for scientists to study the topic. In line with his claim that anxiety and fear must be consciously experienced, he argues that it does not make sense to use the words "fear" or "anxiety" when discussing nonhuman animals. While a dog might avert its gaze from its owner after destroying his newspaper, there is no reason to suspect that the dog is experiencing anything akin to human shame. A rat might flee from a predator, but we have no way to determine what it is "feeling," nor can we determine if it is "feeling" anything at all. As far as we know, these animals lack the ability to recognize their internal experiences, to relate these experiences to their external causes, or to label their subjective experiences verbally.

2. What purpose do fear and anxiety serve?

Charles Darwin hypothesized that fear reactions are present across many types of animals because of the evolutionary advantage they confer on the individual and the species. An antelope that doesn't run from lions is unlikely to live long enough to procreate, and a species that does not respond to danger will not survive. The dodo, a flightless bird that lived on a secluded island off the coast of Madagascar, is an example of an animal whose evolutionary past did not provide it with the tools it needed to survive new challenges. Because the dodo evolved in an environment without natural predators, these birds were not afraid of the humans who visited the island. Within about 100 years of humans' arrival on the island, the dodo went extinct.

The parasite *Toxoplasma gondii* (*toxo* for short) illustrates the consequences for an animal when its threat detection system is interrupted. *Toxo* can only reproduce inside the digestive system of cats and can reach this location only if a cat eats a rodent that is carrying the parasite. To increase its chances of getting into a cat's stomach, *toxo* "rewires" the brains of infected rodents so that they are more likely to be eaten by cats. Under normal circumstances, rats are terrified of the smell of cat urine. A rodent infected with *toxo*, however, becomes sexually attracted to this scent. With its threat detection system hijacked, an infected rodent approaches danger and is eaten by a cat, thereby allowing the *toxo* parasite to reproduce inside its cat host and start the cycle anew.

Through the same process of natural selection that shaped a rodent's usual tendency to avoid cats, humans have been shaped by evolution to activate defensive responses when under threat. For most of our evolutionary history, humans and our hominid ancestors had to contend with a host of imminent physical dangers. Early humans lived in a world in which there was a significant chance of being killed by another member of one's own species, eaten by a predator, or dying of poisoning, dehydration, starvation, or exposure to the elements. To survive, our ancestors developed a series of adaptations for detecting and responding to threats, and the emotions of fear and anxiety are parts of this threat response system.

Consider this list of some common physiological responses to threats and their hypothesized evolutionary purpose:

- Rapid heart rate and deeper, faster breathing: These lead to increased oxygen levels in the blood, which provides fuel for the major muscle groups and improves cognition, allowing the individual to fight or run more effectively.
- Pale skin: The body draws blood toward the skeletal muscles, and away from the skin, to help the individual fight or run. Because there is less blood near the surface of the skin, injuries will result in less blood loss.
- Feeling light-headed or dizzy: The body takes in large amounts of oxygen and blows off carbon dioxide to prepare it to run or fight, which is helpful when a real threat is present. In the case of someone who is not in any imminent danger, this loss of carbon dioxide (which is also known as hyperventilation) provokes the sensation of dizziness and shortness of breath.
- Coldness or tingling in hands and feet: In preparation for fighting or fleeing, the body draws blood from the extremities to the larger muscle groups and internal organs. The tingling sensation and coldness result from the change in blood flow.
- Hairs standing up: In our ancestors who had fur, this would have allowed them to look bigger, which might have convinced their foe to retreat rather than fight. It may also help humans regulate their temperature.
- Dry mouth, nausea, needing to urinate or defecate: The body devotes all of its resources to escaping danger and shuts down all nonessential functions, including digestion. Voiding of the bowels, bladder, and stomach may allow the individual to run faster due to reduced weight.
- Pupils dilate (letting in more light), and hearing becomes more sensitive: These perceptual changes temporarily sharpen the senses,

allowing the individual to quickly scan the environment for threats. Such perceptual experiences are typical in panic attacks, during which the world may appear fuzzy, overly bright, or less real.

- Hot and cold flashes: The body attempts to regulate temperature as it balances multiple biological priorities. Some of these activities may lead the individual to feel warm, while others may cause the person to shiver or feel cold.

- Increased sweat: Researchers have hypothesized that people may sweat to help them maintain a healthy temperature when their racing hearts could otherwise cause them to overheat. Sweating may also make people more slippery, allowing them to evade predators. Furthermore, through transmission via body odor, sweat may also communicate danger to others. In fact, researchers found that when test subjects inside an fMRI scanner smelled cotton swabs that had absorbed the sweat from first-time skydivers, their brains lit up in areas associated with fear but showed no such activation in response to the sweat from people who had been exercising. Interestingly, participants were not able to consciously distinguish between the two types of sweat, even though their brains responded differently to the two sweat samples.

After reviewing the preceding list, it should be obvious that the human body's response to threats (of which the conscious experience of fear is just one aspect) is crucial for survival. Anxiety, which involves worry about a future threat that may or may not materialize, has no easily identifiable benefit. Why would evolution have preserved anxiety if its only apparent effect is to make people miserable?

To answer this question, we must distinguish between two different meanings of the word "anxiety." You may recall that this term can describe a state (meaning a transient response to a potential threat) as well as a trait (meaning a person's general propensity to experience state anxiety across situations). At extremely high levels, neither state nor trait anxiety is likely to be helpful to the individual or the species. However, more moderate state and trait anxiety appears to offer an advantage.

As a trait, anxiety helps people survive by making them more avoidant of potentially dangerous situations. The fearless early human might have gone hunting alone, unafraid of possibly encountering a dangerous rival. His adventurous nature might bring social status and increased mating opportunities, but it could also result in death. The anxious early human, being more cautious, would have preferred the relative safety of hunting in a group. Those low in trait anxiety, unconcerned about losing their status in the group, would have been more likely to challenge the authority of the group's leader. A successful attempt to take power could lead to increased status and reproductive opportunities, but an unsuccessful challenge to move up the hierarchy could result in ostracism from the community, which would eliminate any opportunity to reproduce. Those higher in trait anxiety, owing to their tendency toward imagining future negative consequences, would have passively accepted their position in the social hierarchy. The adventurous may be extolled as heroes, but they don't necessarily survive long enough to reproduce.

The cognitive and physiological aspects of the anxious state can also sometimes be adaptive. Worry about the future, which represents the cognitive component of state anxiety, motivates people to prepare for potential threats. A soldier, concerned that his gun may jam at a moment when he needs it, checks and rechecks to make sure it's in working order. A factory worker, worried about losing his job to downsizing, keeps his full attention focused on the task at hand. A student, unsure if she's ready for a test, wakes up early to study the material one more time.

The physiological arousal that characterizes state anxiety could help people respond to threats. High levels of state anxiety, for example, often make it harder to fall asleep and stay asleep through the night. The resulting wakefulness means that the anxious person is alert and ready to respond to a threat if one arises. Furthermore, when people are in an anxious state, they are more likely to interpret others' facial expressions as hostile. When confronted with someone who means you harm, the rapid recognition of dangerous people can be life-saving.

Research suggests that individuals who are more vulnerable tend to experience higher levels of anxiety. For example, researchers have found that lower birth weight, which is associated with prematurity and physical disability, is also correlated with higher anxiety later in life. People of lower social status, who have fewer resources to cope with negative events and to whom these events are more likely to occur, have higher levels of anxiety. Women, who are more vulnerable to threat than men because they tend to have less physical strength, are more likely to have anxiety disorders than are men. People who live alone, (and who therefore tend to have less social support) also have higher levels of anxiety. Anxiety is more severe among those with chronic illnesses and physical disabilities, as they are less able to deal with threatening events once they occur. From an evolutionary perspective, it makes perfect sense that to ensure their survival, people who are more vulnerable to being harmed by adverse events would need to be more vigilant.

Scientists have identified and studied humans who have specific brain abnormalities that impact their ability to experience fear or anxiety. One such example is a woman, known in the scientific literature as S.M., whose amygdala (a part of the brain that is critical in the processing of fear) was destroyed in childhood by a rare genetic condition. Experiments on S.M. have found that she does not experience fear in response to handling spiders or snakes, from haunted houses, or from watching movie clips that provoke fear in others. In fact, one of the scientists who studied S.M. noted that during an experiment testing her response to snakes, S.M. had to be "restrained from playing with the ones that would actually be quite dangerous to her."

S.M., whom researchers and journalists describe as extremely friendly, is unable to identify fear in others' facial expressions, cannot judge whether strangers are trustworthy, and does not possess the concept of personal space. Unlike people with intact amygdalae, S.M. feels perfectly comfortable standing nose-to-nose with strangers while making eye contact. Likely because of her impaired ability to feel fear and anxiety, S.M. has been the victim of multiple violent attacks by strangers and by her first husband, who nearly beat her to death. Interestingly, researchers have been able to induce panic in S.M. by having her inhale carbon dioxide, which induces a feeling of being starved for air. S.M.'s response to carbon dioxide suggests that there are pathways to fear that don't require a functioning amygdala. (See Question 3 titled "How is the experience of fear 'made' by the brain?" for more information on physiology of fear.)

3. How is the experience of fear "made" by the brain?

You walk down a dark, deserted street late at night. You hear footsteps behind you. Distant at first, the sound seems to be getting closer. Fear washes over you, and you break into a sprint. Your pursuer does the same. Realizing that you can't outrun him, you ready yourself for a fight.

What is happening in your brain that enables this response?

THE TRIUNE BRAIN

The conscious experience that we call "fear" relies on the cooperation of brain systems involved in sensation, perception, arousal, attention, and memory. The "triune brain" model, proposed in the 1960s by the

neuroscientist Paul MacLean (1913–2007), c
accurate) way to think about how the fear re
suggested that the human brain is compris
cialized for certain functions, each of wh
period of evolution.

LAYER 1: THE REPTILIAN (OR PRIMITIVᴇ,

Layer 1, located at the base of the brain, is known as the rept11.
because of its presence in species ranging from lizards to humans. Layeɪ
is responsible for regulating vital functions, including heart rate, temperature, hunger, and balance. When you run, layer 1 senses the change and
directs your heart rate to increase, your skin to dissipate heat through
perspiration, and your respiratory system to take in more air.

The activity of systems falling under the control of layer 1 is autonomic
(i.e., automatic). These regions of the brain and their connections that
run down the spine and into the body are therefore known as the "autonomic nervous system." The autonomic nervous system is made up of two
parts: the sympathetic nervous system (SNS) and parasympathetic nervous system (PNS). The SNS is recruited in times of stress and is involved
in the "fight, flight, or freeze" response. The PNS, by contrast, is responsible for the body's "rest and digest" functions and restores calm when the
SNS stops sounding the alarms. The SNS can be thought of as the gas
pedal and the PNS as the brakes.

LAYER 2: THE LIMBIC SYSTEM
(OR MAMMALIAN BRAIN)

MacLean dubbed this layer the limbic system (also known as the mamma-
lian brain), and it is involved in generating emotions. This layer, which
evolved and expanded in mammals, sits atop the reptilian brain. When
you hear footsteps approaching rapidly, layer 2, detecting a threat, sends a
message to layer 1, which commands your heart rate to increase.

LAYER 3: THE NEOCORTEX

This layer, known as the neocortex, is the outermost layer of the brain and
is the most recently evolved. The neocortex exists across mammal species,
but it is proportionally larger in primates than in other species. The neocortex is especially large in humans, accounting for 76 percent of human brain

r 3 houses the functions—including abstract reasoning, mem-
nt, and language—that we commonly think of as the mind.

y reading a story about someone being chased through a dark
an lead to elevated heart rate: layer 3 interprets the meaning of the
and signals layer 2 to make you feel fear, which in turn signals layer 1
generate an increase in heart rate.

COMMUNICATION AMONG LAYERS OF THE BRAIN

The brain is organized in such a way that communication is not simply top-down (level 3 signals level 2, which signals level 1), but also
bottom-up (level 2 can signal level 3; level 1 can signal levels 2 and 3).
One of the most fascinating examples of this, described by biologist
Robert Sapolsky in his 2017 book *Behave*, was a study that demonstrated
that subjects were more likely to describe a person as cold if he or she
had recently held a cold drink and were more likely to judge a person
as warm if he or she had just held a hot drink. Temperature, processed
in level 1, impacted conscious evaluative thought, which is processed
in level 3.

When there is a conflict between level 1 and level 3, level 1 ultimately
wins. To demonstrate this fact, take a look at a clock, and hold your breath
for as long as possible. Most people can last for about 30 to 60 seconds
before gasping for air. No matter how hard level 3 tries to resist the urge,
level 1, detecting the buildup of carbon dioxide in the bloodstream, will
eventually force you to breathe. Another example can be observed among
people who faint in response to seeing blood or getting a flu shot. In such
people, the sight of blood triggers a reaction in level 1, which shuts down
conscious activity in level 3.

With a bit of practice, most people can learn to apply breathing and
other relaxation strategies to reduce the activity of the sympathetic nervous system, which reflects a process of using conscious thoughts arising from level 3 to control physiological arousal emanating from level 1.
A more extreme example of the way in which mental activity in level 3
can control the physiological activity in level 1 is observed among Bud-
dhist monks trained in a form of yoga known as g-tummo. With many
years of experience in g-tummo, these monks learn to use a breathing
technique that raises their body temperatures several degrees and to prevent heat loss by focusing on a mental image of flames running along their
spinal cords. To be sure, this is an amazing accomplishment, but it also
demonstrates how difficult it can be to use conscious thought to control
level 1 processes.

LOW ROAD AND HIGH ROAD

According to the leading anxiety researcher Joseph LeDoux, the brain does not have a single, unified "fear circuit" that is responsible for producing defensive behaviors as well as the subjective experience of fear (i.e., "feeling scared"). Instead, the brain has two routes by which a threat signal can initiate a response. LeDoux labeled these pathways the *low road* and the *high road*. The low road, using level 1 and level 2, operates outside of consciousness. It is fast but prone to errors. The high road runs through level 3 and involves parts of the brain responsible for conscious thought and decision-making. The high road is slower than the low road, but it is more accurate. While the low road can initiate nonconscious defensive responses, the high road is responsible for the subjective (i.e., conscious) experience of fear.

Defensive behaviors, otherwise known as the "fight–flight–freeze" response, are generated through the low road. These defensive actions arise from level 1 and level 2, which, after interpreting information from the senses, determine that there is no time to wait for the conscious deliberation of level 3. If you have ever had to swerve to avoid getting into a car accident, you may have noticed that you reacted before you had time to consciously apprehend what was happening. If level 3 had gotten involved in this process, you might have thought about how rapidly the other car was approaching, how much damage you could expect to incur, whether the other driver seemed likely to respond to you beeping your horn, and so on. By the time you worked your way through the pros and cons of various reactions, it would have been too late to avoid a crash.

The low road produces defensive reactions through the following sequence:

1. The visual image of the approaching car is sent to a level 2 brain structure called the thalamus, which acts as a relay system that directs sensory information to the appropriate part of the brain.
2. The thalamus, which does not know how to evaluate the meaning of the visual data, passes the signal to the amygdala, an almond-shaped structure located in level 2 that is particularly critical for the expression of fear and aggression. The amygdala collects information from all of the senses, but it is also connected to "higher-order" brain regions that are responsible for attention and conscious thought (level 3).
3. If the signal is consistent with a dangerous object (e.g., a visual pattern that resembles a snake), the amygdala sends a signal to the hypothalamus. The hypothalamus is a small structure located above the

brain stem (level 1) and below the thalamus (level 2). The hypothalamus, which acts as a communications hub, is the place where parts of
the brain responsible for emotion talk to parts of the brain responsible
for core regulation (level 1).

4. The hypothalamus releases a hormone—a chemical messenger that
    travels through the body—called corticotropin-releasing hormone
    (CRH).

5. The release of CRH triggers the pituitary gland to release another
    hormone, adrenocorticotropic hormone (ACTH), which travels
    through the bloodstream to the adrenal glands, located on top of the
    kidneys.

6. The adrenal glands release adrenaline and cortisol into the blood-
    stream. The release of cortisol results in higher levels of glucose in the
    blood, which in combination with adrenaline, leads to heightened
    arousal and provides the increased energy needed to fight or flee.

Simultaneous with the signal traveling the low road, another signal takes the slower route along the high road. The first two steps of
the high road sequence are the same as those of the low road: sensory
information goes to the thalamus and then to the amygdala. While
the low road transmits a danger signal from the amygdala directly
to the hypothalamus, in the high road, the amygdala passes the signal
to the prefrontal cortex (level 3), which is responsible for the conscious
assessment of danger. The prefrontal cortex examines the stimulus in
detail and, in consultation with an area of the brain that stores memory,
determines whether the stimulus is actually dangerous. If the prefrontal
cortex determines that the danger is real, it signals the amygdala to keep
sounding the alarms. If it determines that there is no danger, the prefrontal cortex tells the amygdala to stop sounding the alarms, thereby
terminating the physiological component of fear and returning the body
to its equilibrium state. Anxiety disorders can result either from having
an overly sensitive limbic system, which triggers the body's defenses in
the absence of danger, or from having a prefrontal cortex that fails to
terminate the fear response.

4. How do fear and anxiety affect our physiology, subjective experience, and behavior?

After getting food poisoning from sushi several years earlier, Amy, worried
that she would get ill again, developed an aversion to eating at restaurants.

Though it caused some difficulty in her social life, Amy had been able to avoid restaurants for the last three years. Unfortunately, Amy's boss invited her to a birthday party, and she felt obligated to attend. In the days leading up to the event, Amy noticed occasional queasiness and difficulty sleeping, but these symptoms became more pronounced when the event drew nearer. On her way to the restaurant, she began to feel faint and wondered if she was already ill. "I probably shouldn't go to the party if I'm sick," she thought. Worried about the repercussions if she canceled on her boss, Amy decided that she'd better attend.

After hesitating by the door, she pushed herself to enter the restaurant. Noticing a "weird smell," she broke out in a sweat. As she scanned the tables to find her group, she observed that her colleagues were seated far from the bathroom. Amy worried that she wouldn't have time to get from the table to the restroom if she got sick and imagined the humiliation she'd feel if this happened. She watched as a waiter accidentally touched a piece of bread with his bare hands. She experienced a wave of nausea and became sure that she would get sick if she stayed even one minute longer. Amy rushed to the door, hoping that her boss hadn't seen her.

As illustrated in this example, fear and anxiety can be powerful forces, but how do they exert their effects?

The psychologist Peter Lang proposed that fear is made up of components arising from three different response systems: physiological, subjective, and behavioral. The physiological element refers to autonomic arousal associated with the "fight–flight–freeze" response; the subjective facet refers to the way in which someone describes his or her emotional experience (e.g., "I'm feeling terrified"); and the behavioral aspect is demonstrated by avoidance and escape behaviors. We will review these domains in this chapter.

PHYSIOLOGICAL

The activation of the defensive survival circuits leads to a cascade of physiological changes meant to promote survival. (See Question 3 titled "How is the experience of fear 'made' by the brain?" for more information on the physiology of fear.) These changes include nonconscious physiological responses as well as the conscious awareness of fear or anxiety that is made possible by functions carried out by the body and brain. When the intensity of fear matches the situation, it promotes survival. Similarly, when it is appropriate to the threat, increased arousal provides the alertness one needs to cope with a challenge. (See Question 17 titled "How does anxiety cause people to 'choke' under pressure?" for more information on the role of arousal.)

In the previous example, Amy's anxiety—as manifested by intense physical symptoms—is clearly not helping her adapt to her circumstances. Beginning weeks before the dinner, but increasing as the date approached, Amy's anxiety placed her in a state of chronic arousal, making it difficult for her to sleep. Unfortunately, sleep deprivation is both a consequence and a cause of anxiety and can fuel anxiety even in those who do not typically suffer from it.

As her distress intensified, Amy felt faint and became sweaty, and when her nausea increased to a level she couldn't tolerate, she felt compelled to escape. Like sleep disturbances, nausea can be both a symptom and cause of anxiety. During anxious arousal, the sympathetic nervous system "takes over the controls" to enable an effective response to whatever emergency has tripped the body's alarm systems. All resources are diverted to dealing with the threat, so nonessential activities, including those related to growth, reproduction, and digestion, are temporarily suspended.

At the low end of intensity, anxiety can lead to the experience of "butterflies in your stomach," which is familiar to most people. However, when stress becomes severe and chronic, it can lead to serious digestive conditions. The link between anxiety and gastric problems is supported by research that shows a strong relationship between irritable bowel syndrome (IBS), and anxiety disorders. One study, for example, found that 41 percent of patients with panic disorder also had IBS.

BEHAVIORAL

There is some overlap among the behavioral manifestations of fear and anxiety, but each will be treated separately due to some significant differences. Here, we define a behavior as an action that is observable to others. While a thought would not qualify as a behavior under this definition, a statement made by someone describing that thought would be considered a behavior.

As previously discussed, the emotion of fear is one component of the body's threat response system. When an imminent threat emerges, humans (and many other animals) have three behavioral options available: fight, flight, or freeze. Research using rats suggests that several factors impact which behavioral response is selected. After a rat detects a predator, its default response is to freeze, as this may help the rat avoid alerting the predator to its presence. If the predator detects the rat and starts to approach, the rat may either fight or flee. The rat selects its response based on the proximity of the predator, whether the environment is one that supports escape, the dangerousness of the predator, and whether the rat has family members to protect.

Under certain circumstances, fainting may be an adaptive response, as someone who faints after sustaining an injury will lose less blood due to reduced heart rate and blood pressure. There is some evidence that humans, like other animals, sometimes respond to direct contact with a predator or an overpowering enemy by becoming paralyzed and numb to pain (note that this is different from fainting because there is no loss of consciousness during this paralytic state). Such responses are sometimes described by survivors of rape, who report that their bodies went completely limp during the attack. Some experts have theorized that complete stillness and immobility might reduce the risk of injury from physical aggression during a rape, as it may signal to an attacker that the victim does not need to be subdued with further violence.

Because anxiety involves a threat that is neither certain nor imminent, there is greater variability in how people respond to anxiety as compared to fear. Anxiety can motivate effective problem-solving behavior to reduce the odds of future negative consequences. Anxiety about an upcoming test, for example, could lead someone to study harder. Anxiety about one's health could motivate someone to maintain positive eating and sleep habits.

However, anxiety can also lead to avoidance behaviors, which reflect the attempts of the anxious person to stay away from the feared situation, object, or internal experience. Avoidant behaviors can take several forms, including cognitive avoidance (trying to distract oneself from thoughts that provoke distress), behavioral avoidance (steering clear of people, situations, and objects that evoke anxiety), reassurance-seeking behaviors (asking others repeatedly to say things that reduce one's anxiety), and interoceptive avoidance behaviors (abstaining from physical activities that elicit uncomfortable internal states).

Safety behaviors represent a subtler form of avoidance that may not be immediately obvious to an observer. When someone engages in a safety behavior, he or she may get themselves to attend a party that provokes social anxiety, or may drive to work despite the fear of having a panic attack, but he or she can do so only by engaging in behaviors that are intended to prevent the feared outcome. Examples could include someone with agoraphobia who will leave the house only if he carries antianxiety medicine with him at all times, someone with social anxiety who makes phone calls only if she writes down everything she plans to say verbatim before calling, and someone with obsessive-compulsive disorder (OCD) who checks the lock on his home repeatedly to reassure himself that his house won't be burglarized.

SUBJECTIVE

The subjective aspects of fear and anxiety are manifested by a person's verbal report. The presence of elevated heart rate and behavioral avoidance do not necessarily prove that someone is feeling fear or anxiety since these reactions can also appear when someone is disgusted or angry. Though physiological arousal and avoidance are often prominent components of fear and anxiety, a person's verbal report is the one essential piece of evidence that establishes whether he or she is feeling these emotions.

Intuitively, it is sensible to expect that heightened arousal, increased subjective distress, and avoidance of the feared object should "go together." Interestingly, however, the three components of fear sometimes show little correspondence with one another. Someone may, for example, report that they are feeling very scared but remain outwardly calm. Indeed, this is often the case for people who fear public speaking, who may be surprised to hear from audience members that—despite experiencing high distress during the speech—they seemed entirely at ease. On the other hand, someone else might report low subjective fear but show significant physiological signs of arousal. Indeed, research suggests that following successful treatment for anxiety disorders, people tend to show reduced avoidance and lower levels of subjective distress, but their physiological reactions to stress (e.g., increase in heart rate in situations that used to provoke high anxiety) do not tend to change as much following treatment.

5. How do fear and anxiety impact perception and cognition?

Anxiety and fear change the way people process information by diverting their attention toward whatever is eliciting their emotional response. When people feel fear, they become hypervigilant to threats. They scan the environment rapidly to identify potential sources of danger and then narrow their focus if a threat is located. The narrowing of attention enhances the sensitivity of perception; sounds can seem louder, and vision can become sharper.

Consider a man with an intense fear of airplanes, seated on a flight next to his nonfearful wife. Due to his fear, the man's attention is easily grabbed by stimuli, such as even minor turbulence, that signal threat. Fear hijacks his thoughts, and though he tries to distract himself with a crossword puzzle, his mind keeps providing him with new evidence that the plane is going to crash. He notices a high-pitched sound coming from the engine outside his window and thinks, "that's not a normal sound—there's definitely something wrong with this plane." He asks his wife if she can hear it, but she says that she cannot. As his fear climbs, the man becomes increasingly likely to misinterpret ambiguous information as a sign of danger. After a rough jolt of turbulence (to which his wife bravely responds by falling asleep), the man looks at the flight attendant. "She seems nervous. She must know that this flight is doomed."

As illustrated by the man who hears sounds emanating from the engine that are inaudible to others, the intensification of the senses under conditions of fear can lead to perceptual distortions. One study, for example, found that people standing on a skateboard at the top of a hill, which generated fear, perceived the slant as steeper than those who stood on a cardboard box. Another study on people with a specific phobia of spiders (commonly known as arachnophobia) found that people who reported high levels of fear perceived the spiders as larger than those who experienced lower levels of fear.

Similar results were found for perceptions of height. Researchers demonstrated that when people were shown an object some number of feet ahead of them, they estimated the distance with good accuracy. However, when participants stood on a high balcony and were asked to estimate the distance to the ground (which was identical to their distance from the object that was ahead of them), they tended to estimate that the distance to the ground was much greater.

Fear also influences perceptions of proximity and motion. One study found that when looking at a brief video of a snake or a spider moving toward them, people underestimated how long it would take for the animal to collide with them. Participants did not make the same error when the video featured a nonthreatening animal like a rabbit or butterfly. This effect was especially pronounced in people who were afraid of snakes and spiders, presumably because higher levels of fear led to more significant distortions in their perceptions of time and distance.

Though anxiety and fear make people more likely to overestimate risk, these emotions have somewhat different effects on cognition. Under conditions of fear, when there is a clearly identified source of danger, mental activity focuses on determining the best course of action to deal with the threat. When arousal is low to moderate, the prefrontal cortex (the part of the brain responsible for conscious decision-making) maintains control. Behaviors undertaken through this process are deliberate, as the prefrontal cortex can inhibit the impulsive responses arising from the more primitive emotional centers of the brain. When arousal is intense, the prefrontal cortex goes quiet, and the amygdala takes control. The hand-off of control from conscious deliberation to intuitive responding explains why after acts of heroism, people typically report that they acted without thinking. (See Question 3 titled "How is the experience of fear 'made' by the brain?" for more information on the neural processing of fear.)

Unlike fear, anxiety involves a threat that may not be truly danger-ous and that may not even occur. Due to its uncertain nature, anxiety is characterized by worry thoughts, which center on possible adverse future events and how the individual might deal with them. To the extent that it helps someone anticipate a likely problem and work on finding a solution, worry can be productive. Worry becomes ineffective when it is accompa-nied by intense anxiety, which interferes with critical thinking, disrupts planning, and leaves the person feeling less competent to deal with the future challenge. In anxiety-provoking situations, people may also imag-ine future adverse events in detail (e.g., vividly imagining what it would feel like to be in a plane crash). Such imagery increases people's estima-tions of the probability of the feared event and thereby contributes to increased anxiety.

6. What is a panic attack?

As defined by the *DSM-5*, a panic attack is "an abrupt surge of intense fear or intense discomfort that reaches a peak within minutes." To be consid-ered a true panic attack by the *DSM-5*, someone must experience at least 4 out of 13 possible symptoms. The first ten of these symptoms describe different forms of physical discomfort, such as shortness of breath, heart palpitations, feelings of choking, chest pain, and numbness or tingling. The final three symptoms relate more to the individual's cognitive experi-ence and include dissociation (i.e., feeling disconnected from reality), fear of losing control or "going crazy," and most distressingly, the fear of dying.

Panic attacks are classified as *expected* when there is an identifiable trigger for the panic, or as *unexpected* when there is no obvious trigger. Unexpected panic attacks, which must be present for a diagnosis of panic disorder, have no clear trigger and are experienced as coming "out of the blue." One study found that in comparison to panic disorder, which has a lifetime prevalence of about 3 percent, panic attacks are experienced by about one-third of the population at some point in their lives.

Panic attacks generally reach their peak within a few minutes, but they can also last over an hour and may sometimes come in waves over the course of several hours. Even after a panic attack has ended, the individual may feel fatigued and have difficulty focusing or interacting with others. Though the individual experiencing a panic attack feels overwhelmed by fear, he or she may also develop the ability to hide his or her anxiety from others, and those around him or her may be unaware that the individual is feeling anxious at all.

It is not yet clear what causes panic attacks, but psychiatrist Donald Klein has proposed that panic attacks are caused by a "false alarm" in the brain. In this theory, evolution has provided humans with a suffocation alarm system, which alerts us if an abnormal amount of carbon dioxide is detected. This may explain why people experience "air hunger" during panic attacks, which refers to the distressing experience of gasping for breath and feeling that one can't get enough air. Air hunger is a common symptom of panic attacks but is rarely seen when people experience other kinds of fear initiated by external danger. This theory would also explain why panic attacks are more common among smokers and those with pulmonary problems.

Interestingly, recent research suggests that although some panic attack sufferers may describe their panic as coming out of nowhere, physiological changes can be detected for at least an hour before they become aware that a panic attack has begun. This study found that in the hour before a panic attack, there was an increase in carbon dioxide levels and greater instability in other physiological areas that did not occur outside of episodes of panic. This research also offers an explanation as to why treatments that focus on normalizing the breathing patterns of panic attack sufferers are helpful, as such treatments would prevent the buildup of carbon dioxide that seems to trigger panic attacks.

7. What are the different kinds of anxiety disorders?

Anxiety disorders are a group of psychiatric conditions that are characterized by distress and/or impairment due to disproportionately high levels of fear and anxiety. The anxiety disorders listed in the *DSM-5* include separation anxiety disorder, selective mutism (SM), specific phobia, social anxiety disorder (SAD), panic disorder, agoraphobia, and generalized anxiety disorder (GAD). Obsessive-compulsive disorder (OCD) and post-traumatic stress disorder (PTSD) were categorized as anxiety disorders until the *DSM*'s fifth revision in 2013, which placed these conditions into separate diagnostic groups. Though they are no longer classified as anxiety disorders, they share anxiety as an essential characteristic and are therefore reviewed in Question 8 titled "Are there other mental disorders that have anxiety as a key characteristic?" The coming sections will provide an overview of these conditions (Table 1).

Table 1 Anxiety Disorders and Their Key Characteristics

Anxiety Disorder	Key Characteristic
Separation anxiety disorder	Anxiety and/or fear about separating from an attachment figure
Selective mutism	Consistent failure to speak in certain social situations despite being able to speak in other situations
Specific phobia	Anxiety/fear/avoidance of specific objects or situations
Social anxiety disorder	Anxiety/fear/avoidance of social situations in which there is a risk of being judged negatively by others
Panic disorder	Recurrent unexpected panic attacks that lead to worry and maladaptive behavioral changes to reduce the risk of future panic attacks
Agoraphobia	Anxiety/fear about being stuck in a fear-inducing situation that can't easily be escaped
Generalized anxiety disorder	Uncontrollable anxiety and worry about a variety of issues, coupled with physiological symptoms of anxious arousal
Obsessive-compulsive disorder*	Presence of recurrent, unwanted thoughts that provoke distress (obsessions) and repetitive behaviors aimed at reducing the distress (compulsions)
Post-traumatic stress disorder*	Physiological, emotional, cognitive, and behavioral symptoms that arise in response to a traumatic event

*Not classified as an anxiety disorder in *DSM-5*.

Source: Adapted from American Psychiatric Association. (2013). *Diagnostic and statistical manual of mental disorders* (5th ed.). Arlington, VA: American Psychiatric Publishing.

Anxiety disorders share several traits, including a bias toward paying attention to stimuli that signal a threat, heightened anxiety/fear in response to such signals, and a tendency to interpret ambiguous information as threatening. Anxiety disorders also manifest themselves in similar ways, in that they are associated with avoidance of the feared object or situation. What distinguishes someone with panic disorder from someone with social anxiety disorder, or someone with PTSD from someone with a specific phobia, are two factors: (1) the situation(s) that elicit the problematic emotional response and (2) the content of the anxiety-related thoughts and beliefs.

An example should offer some clarity. Imagine that Albert, a 16-year-old boy, has been refusing to leave his home for several months due to anxiety. Which anxiety disorder does he have? The diagnosis depends on what Albert is avoiding (i.e., the stimuli that are evoking distress) and the thoughts that are driving his emotional response. If Albert is afraid of having a panic attack outside his home, he could have agoraphobia and possibly panic disorder. If he worries about being judged negatively by his peers, he may have social anxiety disorder. If Albert fears being bitten by a neighbor's dog, he probably has a specific phobia. If he is afraid of stepping on a crack in the sidewalk because it may cause harm to a family member, he is likely to have OCD. If Albert was the victim of an assault and suffers extreme fear when memories of this event are triggered, he probably has PTSD. Of course, if Albert lives in a part of the world with ongoing violence and has good reason to fear for his safety, then his behavior may be adaptive, and no diagnosis is applicable.

SEPARATION ANXIETY DISORDER

Separation anxiety disorder is characterized by excessive fear or anxiety related to separating from home or from people to whom the individual is attached. This diagnosis is most often made in infants and young children, though it can be applied to adults as well. Separation anxiety disorder often develops following a stressful life event, such as the death of a loved one or pet, moving to a new neighborhood, divorce of parents, or for adolescents and adults, transitioning to a new stage of life.

While it is normal for children to experience some anxiety when they are separating from parents, the diagnosis is applied only when the child's anxiety exceeds what would normally be expected given his or her developmental level. For example, while you would expect a three-year-old to cry when he or she is being dropped off at day care, such behavior would obviously be a concern if the child were in high school. Children with separation anxiety disorder might avoid school or refrain from socializing with peers and may experience negative consequences as a result.

Individuals with separation anxiety disorder worry that something bad may happen that will prevent them from being able to see their loved one again (e.g., the child fears that he or she will be kidnapped or that a parent may get into a car accident). These fears may cause a child to avoid being alone or refuse to leave home without a parent. The child may have difficulty falling asleep without a parent in the room. Individuals with separation anxiety disorder may also develop physical symptoms, such as headaches and gastric complaints, when they anticipate separation from attachment figures or when separation occurs.

According to the DSM-5, separation anxiety disorder is the most common anxiety disorder among children under the age of 12, with a 6-to-12-month prevalence of around 4 percent. Separation anxiety disorder becomes less prevalent in adolescence, with a 12-month prevalence in the United States of 1.6 percent, and is least common among adults, in whom there is a 12-month prevalence of 0.9 percent to 1.9 percent. The course of separation anxiety disorder doesn't tend to follow a linear path, and those with this disorder frequently experience periods of remission and exacerbation. Such recurrences typically occur in the context of a life-stage transition, such as graduating high school.

SELECTIVE MUTISM

Selective mutism (SM) is diagnosed in children who—despite having the ability to speak in some situations—persistently fail to speak in specific social situations in which speech would normally be expected. Individuals with SM vary with regard to the situations in which they can and cannot speak. For example, some children will talk openly with close family members but not with peers, while others will speak with peers but not with adults or those who are perceived as being in positions of authority.

SM was first identified as a clinical disorder in 1877 by Adolf Kussmaul (1822–1902), who named the condition *aphasia voluntaria*. Kussmaul's characterization of this condition as being caused by a voluntary refusal to speak was reflected by the inclusion of "elective mutism" as a diagnosis in the third edition of the DSM (1980), which defined the disorder as a "continuous refusal to speak in almost all social situations." In the DSM-IV (1994), the diagnosis was relabeled as "selective mutism" to emphasize the idea that the problem occurs in select (i.e., specific) settings and to avoid the implication that the child is oppositional and is simply choosing not to speak.

While the typical age of onset for SM is thought to be between two and five years, it is often not diagnosed until later in childhood when the child is unable to meet the increased social demands of school. Because children with SM are often talkative in the home, parents are frequently unaware of the problem until teachers inform them. Failure to speak at school can lead to academic difficulties, as teachers may believe that the child with SM does not understand the material and because the child with SM loses the opportunity to ask questions or to read aloud.

The *DSM-5* states that SM is "relatively rare," and that depending on the setting where it is being assessed, it has been found to affect between 0.03 and 1 percent of children. Given the low number of people with this disorder and changing definitions of the diagnosis, the typical course of SM is unknown at this time, though researchers have found that problems with social anxiety are likely to persist even after children with SM "outgrow" their mutism. In fact, some experts have proposed that SM is not a distinct disorder and is a severe form of social anxiety seen in children.

SPECIFIC PHOBIA

Specifc phobia is a diagnosis assigned to those who experience excessive fear or anxiety when confronted with a particular situation or object. Specific phobia is diagnosed when the fear, anxiety, or avoidance causes "clinically significant" distress or leads to impairment in an important area of functioning. In some cases, people with specific phobias may deny that they experience fear or anxiety because they have changed their routines to avoid the feared object or situation entirely. Sometimes, avoiding the feared situation might not be too disruptive (e.g., a person is afraid of bridges, but there is a tunnel that is equally convenient). In other cases, people may be forced to stop doing things they love or to forgo opportunities (e.g., someone must end a relationship because he would have to drive across a bridge to meet his girlfriend).

The *DSM-5* divides specific phobias into five groups based on the "phobic stimulus," meaning the situation or object that provokes distress. The five groups include animal type (e.g., dogs, insects), natural environment type (e.g., heights, storms, water), blood-injection-injury type (B-I-I) (e.g., needles, injury, having blood drawn), situational type (e.g., enclosed spaces, airplanes), and other type (e.g., situations that could lead to vomiting or choking, people dressed as certain characters, clowns). The *DSM-5*'s system of dividing phobias into these subtypes has been criticized on numerous grounds, one of which is the lack of clarity in how certain fears should be categorized. Is a fear of the dark considered a natural environment type phobia, or is it situational type? Does a fear of bridges fit best in the category of natural type, since this is the category for a fear of heights, or is it situational?

While some argue that the division of phobias into multiple types is unhelpful, there is good reason to place B-I-I phobia into its own category. Aside from B-I-I phobia, all other fears are associated with accelerated heart rate when the phobic stimulus is presented. B-I-I phobia, by contrast, involves a two-step response characterized by an initial increase in heart rate, followed by a significant reduction in heart rate and a drop in blood pressure, which can result in fainting.

Multiple theories have been proposed to explain why some people faint in response to blood. Research has demonstrated that B-I-I phobia is more common among women than among men, and that the prevalence of B-I-I phobia drops after boys reach puberty, but does not drop in girls. These observations have led to speculation that B-I-I phobia may have been andvantageous to our ancestors and was therefore preserved by evolution. During warfare, those who were not as capable of fighting (i.e., women and children) might have been more likely to survive if they were incapacitated and therefore unable to struggle or fight back. Another hypothesis points to the fact that people who faint due to B-I-I phobia are also likely to faint in other contexts, reflecting some dysfunction in their autonomic nervous systems. In such people, fainting may be a conditioned fear response that develops after other fainting incidents.

Regardless of whether one finds the categories useful, research suggests that some phobias are more common than others. A 2010 meta-analysis found that animal phobias were among the most common phobias across the lifespan, with a lifetime prevalence of 3.3 to 7 percent. Natural environment-type phobias had a lifetime prevalence rate of 3.1 to 5.3 percent; storm phobia had a lifetime prevalence rate of 2.2 to 3.4 percent, and water phobia had a lifetime prevalence rate of 2 to 2.9 percent. The lifetime prevalence rate for B-I-I phobia was 3.2 to 4.5 percent. Among situational-type phobias, the lifetime prevalence rate for flying phobia was 2.5 to 2.9 percent; phobia of enclosed spaces had a prevalence of 3.2 to 3.3 percent, and driving phobia had a prevalence of 0.7 percent.

As is the case with most other anxiety disorders, women are diagnosed with specific phobias about twice as often as men. However, the discrepancy between men and women differs based on the type of phobia. Among women, animal phobias were most common (8.7%), followed by B-I-I phobia (6.4%), situational phobia (6.4%), and natural environment phobia (5.3%). In men, B-I-I phobia was the most common (3.9%), followed by natural environment phobia (3.2%), animal phobia (2.1%), and situational phobia (1.6%).

When all types of specific phobia are included, research suggests that the mean age of onset is around ten years, but some phobias tend to develop earlier than others. A 2010 review of the literature found that animal phobia tends to start at around age 8, followed by B-I-I phobia at around age 9, natural environment phobia at around age 13, and situational phobia, which tends to develop in adolescence and young adulthood.

It is not known why there is so much variability in when different phobias develop, but it is clear that having a phobia in childhood increases the risk of later problems with anxiety. One study found that a child who has a phobia at age six is five times more likely to have social anxiety disorder in adolescence, and is more than twice as likely to develop depression as an adult.

SOCIAL ANXIETY DISORDER

Individuals are diagnosed with social anxiety disorder (SAD) if they experience significant anxiety or fear in response to social situations during which they may be evaluated negatively by others. This fear may occur across many different social contexts, or it may only happen under specific conditions when the individual must perform in public. Fear of public speaking would be an example of such a "performance-only" form of SAD. People with SAD may experience even the most mundane social interactions—asking for directions, making small talk in an elevator, ordering food in a restaurant—as a source of intense emotional distress.

The diagnosis of SAD requires that the fear or anxiety must be out of proportion to the actual threat posed by the situation. For example, if a child with a speech impediment is too anxious to give a presentation to his class after having recently been bullied about stuttering, he would not be diagnosed with SAD because his fears are well founded and may be proportional to the situation. More typically though, people with SAD tend to assume that they will be judged negatively by others and often predict that these judgments will have catastrophic consequences (e.g., "I'll get fired," or "they'll think I'm a loser and never talk to me again"). At the same time, those with SAD are often aware that their anxiety is disproportionate to the situation, but they feel powerless to control their emotional reactions.

Those with SAD are often particularly fearful that others will notice their anxiety. There is a cruel irony to this fact, as the fear of being perceived as anxious leads to symptoms of anxiety that can be seen by others. Worrying that their awkwardness or anxiety will expose them as weak, weird, or incompetent, people with SAD become hypervigilant to any sign that their emotion is rising to the surface. This vigilance leads them to notice subtle physiological sensations ("I'm starting to blush"), which leads to anxiety-provoking interpretations ("I look so stupid!"), which then exacerbate the symptoms of anxiety the person is trying to conceal (i.e., causes increased blushing).

Social anxiety diverts attention away from the external environment and toward monitoring one's thoughts, physiological experiences, and behaviors. Fear of appearing socially awkward, for example, makes someone with SAD pay close attention to aspects of his or her behavior and appearance that could be judged by others. This could include the sound of one's voice ("Did that sound weird? Am I talking too loud?"), body posture and movements ("Where do I put my hands when I'm not holding a drink? In my pockets? Both hands, or just one hand?"), facial signals ("How long am I supposed to make eye contact for? Is this too short or too long? Am I smiling in a normal way, or is this creepy?"), and the reactions of others ("She's looking around the room instead of at me—is she getting bored? Could she tell that I was making a joke?"). Understandably, having all of these thoughts in rapid succession makes it difficult for people with SAD to focus on the conversation itself and may lead to less engagement from their conversational partner.

Unfortunately, the attempts made by those with SAD to avoid being judged negatively sometimes lead them to act in ways that inadvertently generate negative judgments by others. For example, those with social anxiety may decline invitations to parties, stand at a distance from others at a social event, avoid eye contact during conversations, or look at their phones to escape uncomfortable silences. Others can easily misinterpret these behaviors as signs that the socially anxious person is not interested in speaking with them, and they may judge the person with social anxiety as rude, arrogant, or aloof.

SAD has been called a "disorder of lost opportunities," as efforts to avoid the pain of social rejection or embarrassment can cause people to abandon important goals and to miss out on valuable experiences. People with social anxiety disorder may have difficulty forming and maintaining friendships and are also more likely to drop out of school, to have problems with employment, to have lower income, and to be never-married or divorced. The fear of being perceived negatively may lead those with SAD to avoid a range of activities. Someone whose voice trembles when anxious might avoid talking in social situations, someone who sweats might avoid physical contact, and someone whose hands shake might avoid eating or drinking in the presence of others.

Researchers have found that people with SAD typically report that they have few friendships and that they tend to describe these relationships as being of a lower quality than those without social anxiety. Interestingly, recent research suggests that while people with SAD may experience their friendships as being weak, their nonanxious friends perceive the relationships more positively. This study offers the hopeful message for social anxiety sufferers that their friends probably like them more than they believe.

According to the *DSM-5*, the median age of onset for social anxiety disorder in the United States is 13 years. According to the National Institute of Mental Health (NIMH), the 12-month prevalence for social anxiety disorder among adults in the United States is 6.8 percent, and for adolescents in the United States aged 13–18, the 12-month prevalence is 5.5 percent.

Despite the high levels of distress and dysfunction caused by SAD, about half of those with social anxiety disorder in Western cultures never seek treatment. Those who do eventually get treatment tend to do so after experiencing symptoms for 15–20 years. The lack of help-seeking among those with social anxiety makes sense given the fact that asking for help can trigger the very anxiety for which the person needs treatment.

PANIC DISORDER

Panic disorder is diagnosed in people who experience recurrent panic attacks that are of the unexpected type (defined later in the chapter). A panic attack is characterized by a sudden elevation of fear or physical discomfort, which might involve rapid heart rate or chest pain. A panic attack reaches its peak intensity within a few minutes, and it is accompanied by a variety of physical symptoms (e.g., rapid heart rate) and fear-based thoughts (e.g., "I'm going to die"). To qualify for this diagnosis, an individual must experience at least one month of persistent worry about having another panic attack and/or at least one month during which the individual responds to the panic attack in a way that is maladaptive, such as by refusing to leave the house. It has been estimated that about one-third of Americans experience a panic attack over the course of their lives, but only 10 percent of those who have a panic attack go on to develop panic disorder. (See Question 6 titled "What is a panic attack?" for a more detailed definition of panic attacks.)

Panic disorder is diagnosed only when an individual has recurrent panic attacks that are of the *unexpected* variety. In contrast to an *expected panic attack*, which occurs in response to a known cue, an *unexpected panic attack* happens without any clear trigger. Thus, by the *DSM-5*'s definition, an individual who only experiences panic attacks with a specific and identified trigger would not be diagnosed with panic disorder, regardless of how frequently they happen or how impairing his or her panic attacks may be.

Unexpected panic attacks can happen when an individual is already anxious, but they may also happen without any warning at all, such as when the person feels relaxed or when he or she is waking up in the morning. Being unsure of what triggered their panic attacks, people with panic disorder will often avoid many kinds of activities in an attempt to ensure that they won't have another panic attack or to make sure that they can quickly return to safety. This may lead them to refrain from any kind of physical exertion, to avoid going far away from home, or to abstain from doing anything that causes them even small amounts of anxiety due to fear that they will become overwhelmed and start to panic.

The 12-month prevalence for panic disorder among adults and adolescents in the United States and Europe is approximately 2 to 3 percent. Rates are significantly lower in Asian, African, and Latin American countries, where they range from 0.1 percent to 0.8 percent. Women are about twice as likely to develop panic disorder as men. The usual course of untreated panic disorder is chronic but episodic, with most people experiencing periods of remission and relapse. Full remission, in which an individual goes several years without any panic attacks, is thought to be rare.

Panic disorder is considered relatively rare in children (less than 0.4%), and rates of panic disorder increase over the course of adolescence through early adulthood. The average age of onset for panic disorder is 24 years. The prevalence of panic disorder late in life is lower than in midlife, and it rarely has a new onset among older adults (0.7% of those over the age of 64). It is thought that this decreasing incidence may reflect a general "dampening" of the autonomic nervous system as people reach old age. When people do experience panic attacks for the first time in older age, physicians should look carefully for medical causes or should suspect that the symptoms are due to side effects from medications.

Research has demonstrated that selective serotonin reuptake inhibitor (SSRI) medications are superior to a placebo for treating panic disorder, and SSRIs have been found to reduce the severity of panic symptoms, avoidance of situations that may elicit panic, and frequency of panic attacks. The benefit of SSRIs usually takes 2 to 4 weeks to become evident but can sometimes take 8 to 12 weeks. For many patients, the therapeutic effects can increase over the first 6 to 12 months of SSRI treatment. The positive effects of benzodiazepines are observed much more quickly and can lead to improvement in less than one week. However, due to their potential for abuse and side effects among certain populations, there is some disagreement among experts about the circumstances under which benzodiazepines should be considered. SSRI medications are about equally effective as cognitive-behavioral therapy (CBT) for the treatment of panic disorder, and the combination of CBT and SSRIs is somewhat more effective than either treatment alone.

AGORAPHOBIA

The diagnosis of agoraphobia applies to people who experience high levels of fear, anxiety, or avoidance due to a concern that they will suf-fer panic-like symptoms (or act in an embarrassing manner) when con-fronted with situations in which escape might be difficult or help might be unavailable. As an example, this diagnosis would be given to someone who, having had panic attacks in the past, is afraid to ride the subway because it would be impossible to get off the train quickly if a panic attack were to develop. People with agoraphobia may fear passing out, being trapped, or having a heart attack. Indeed, a 2008 study found that the most common reason for avoidance among those with agoraphobia was the fear that they would become "suddenly incapacitated."

The *DSM-5* requires that someone diagnosed with agoraphobia must experience marked fear or anxiety in at least two out of five situations. These five situations include public transportation, being in open spaces, being in enclosed spaces, being in a crowd or a line, and being alone out-side the home environment. For an individual to receive a diagnosis of agoraphobia, his or her fear or avoidance must be out of proportion to the actual danger posed by the situation.

While it was once thought that agoraphobia occurred only in individu-als who also had panic attacks, recent research has found that a significant number of people with agoraphobia do not have panic attacks. In compar-ison to the *DSM-IV*, which included the diagnosis of "panic disorder with agoraphobia," but did not allow for the diagnosis of agoraphobia as a sep-arate entity, the *DSM-5* now includes a separate diagnosis of agoraphobia, which may be diagnosed regardless of whether the individual experiences panic attacks.

There is a great deal of variation concerning the severity of avoid-ance behaviors in agoraphobia. Some people become so incapacitated by fear that they are entirely homebound, whereas others have much greater mobility. Many people with agoraphobia cope with their anxiety through engaging in "safety behaviors," which are mental or behavioral strategies aimed at reducing the likelihood of a feared event. A safety behavior could include making sure that a friend or family member is always available by phone, carrying antianxiety medication in one's pocket in case of distress, or sitting near the exit of a classroom to enable a quick escape. Such behaviors may be helpful in the short term, but in the long term, they maintain anxiety by preventing the disconfirmation of maladaptive beliefs. If someone with agoraphobia is only willing to leave home when accompanied by a friend, he or she learns that the presence of the friend is the only thing that kept him or her safe, instead of learning that the feared consequence would not have happened even if he or she had been alone.

Regarding prevalence, NIMH estimates that 0.8 percent of adults in the United States suffer from agoraphobia over a 12-month period and that 1.4 percent of U.S. adults have agoraphobia in their lifetimes. Agoraphobia is about twice as common in women than men. It appears to be more common in adolescents, as NIMH estimates that 2.4 percent of adolescents aged 13–18 have agoraphobia. The average age of onset is 20 years; though agoraphobia can occur in children, onset in childhood is thought to be rare. Agoraphobia can have a sudden onset (usually after a panic attack). Onset can also be gradual, as the individual may slowly begin to avoid a wider range of activities and his or her zone of comfort constricts. Unfortunately, researchers have found that when untreated, agoraphobia is extremely persistent, and that complete remission is rare.

GENERALIZED ANXIETY DISORDER

GAD is characterized by excessive and persistent worry and anxiety regarding multiple activities and events that can span across several domains of life. The anxiety and worry are disproportionate to the actual threat posed by the situation and generate significant distress or interfere with the person's ability to function. In contrast to those with panic disorder, who experience an intense and relatively short-lived spike in anxiety, those with GAD are more likely to report a moderate level of anxiety at all times, regardless of the situation.

Noting that most people seem to worry about *something*, one might wonder if this means that everyone would qualify for this diagnosis. The answer is that GAD is quite different from what we would consider "normal worry." Whereas someone with "normal worry" might worry about a single topic, such as his or her grades, someone with GAD would worry about many different issues, such as school performance, health, relationships, and whether he or she will be late for an appointment. Unlike in "normal worry," which might be experienced as tolerable but unpleasant, someone with GAD would experience a level of worry that leads to impairments in his or her ability to work or care for family members. Also, those with GAD are much more likely than those without GAD to have worries that are accompanied by a range of physical symptoms; GAD is common among those with chronic pain that has no identified medical cause.

To further differentiate GAD from "normal worry," the *DSM-5* requires that in addition to anxiety and worry, people must experience at least three of six other symptoms, which include restlessness or feeling "on edge," feeling fatigued easily, problems with concentration, irritability, muscular tension, and sleep difficulties. Unlike adults, who must have at least three of these six symptoms, children only need to have one of the six symptoms to receive a diagnosis of GAD. The *DSM-5* states that the individual must experience these symptoms more days than not for at least six months to earn this diagnosis.

Per the *DSM-5*, the 12-month prevalence of GAD in the United States is 2.9 percent among adults and 0.9 percent among adolescents. Rates of GAD in other countries vary, with some countries having a 12-month prevalence of 0.4 percent, while other countries have a 12-month prevalence of 3.6 percent. Over the course of a lifetime, 9 percent of people will have symptoms sufficient for a diagnosis of GAD. Women are about two times more likely to develop GAD than men. According to NIMH, the average age of onset for GAD in the United States is 31 years of age, which makes GAD the anxiety disorder that tends to develop latest in life. People who develop GAD in adulthood are likely to report that they have been "worriers" since early in life. The symptoms of GAD tend to wax and wane over the course of a lifetime, and full remission is thought to be rare.

8. Are there other mental disorders that have anxiety as a key characteristic?

The *DSM-5* includes the broad category of Anxiety Disorders, which encompasses the conditions that we reviewed in the previous question. The *DSM-5* also introduced two new diagnostic categories: Obsessive-Compulsive and Related Disorders and Trauma and Stressor-Related Disorders. Some of the diagnoses in these groups, such as hoarding disorder and disinhibited social engagement disorder, were not present at all in the *DSM-IV*, while other diagnoses were relocated to these new sections from their previous places.

Consequently, obsessive-compulsive disorder and post-traumatic stress disorder, which previously fell under the heading of Anxiety Disorders, were moved to new categories. Because anxiety is an essential component of these conditions and because research on these diagnoses has contributed to our understanding of anxiety, we include these conditions in our review.

POST-TRAUMATIC STRESS DISORDER

Post-traumatic stress disorder (PTSD) is diagnosed when an individual develops specific physiological, emotional, cognitive, and behavioral symptoms in response to one or more traumatic events. The *DSM-5* defines trauma as "exposure to actual or threatened death, serious injury, or sexual violence," which must be experienced in particular ways. For those aged seven and older to be diagnosed with PTSD, the *DSM-5* requires that the individual must have directly experienced the traumatic event, witnessed the traumatic event in person, learned that the traumatic event happened to a close friend or close family member, or have been exposed to aversive details of the traumatic event. In those aged six and younger, the *DSM-5* includes a preschool subtype to provide a set of criteria that is applicable to young children.

For the first 30 days following a traumatic event, people experiencing post-traumatic stress are diagnosed with acute stress disorder, and their diagnosis is changed to PTSD if symptoms persist 30 days after the trauma. PTSD symptoms usually start to develop in the first three months after a traumatic event, but researchers have found that around 25 percent of those with PTSD developed the disorder six months or more after the incident. In some cases, PTSD may take years to become evident after a trauma. PTSD is often chronic with only one in three recovering after one year and one-third still suffering ten years after the traumatic event. According to the *DSM-5*, the lifetime prevalence of PTSD in the United States is 8.7 percent, and the 12-month prevalence for adults in the United States is 3.5 percent.

The *DSM-5* lists four clusters of symptoms and requires that the individual have at least one symptom from each of these groups to qualify for a diagnosis of PTSD:

- *Intrusive symptoms*: Intrusive symptoms include memories of the traumatic event that are experienced as involuntary and distressing. Nightmares are a common intrusive symptom of PTSD and are reported by up to 90 percent of those with the disorder. Other intrusive symptoms include distress in response to thoughts or external cues that remind the individual of the traumatic event, physiological reactions to cues associated with the trauma, and dissociative symptoms. These dissociative symptoms include depersonalization and derealization. In depersonalization, the person feels detached from his or her own body, and in derealization, the individual feels that the external world is not real.

- *Avoidance*: People with PTSD may attempt to avoid memories, thoughts, and feelings associated with the traumatic event and may try to avoid external cues (e.g., places, objects, people) that elicit unpleasant memories.
- *Negative alterations in mood and cognitions*: This cluster includes an inability to remember important aspects of the traumatic event; extremely negative beliefs about others, the world, or oneself; distorted beliefs that justify self-blame or blame of others for the incident; a persistent negative mood state; reduced interest or engagement in important activities; feeling detached from others; and a persistent lack of positive emotion.
- *Arousal*: Symptoms in this cluster include irritability and outbursts of anger in response to small stressors, self-destructive or dangerous behaviors, hypervigilance, high startle response or jumpiness, difficulties with concentration, and problems falling or staying asleep.

A study in the United States found that while 65 percent of adult participants had been exposed to events that could qualify as a trauma, only 12 percent of these people developed PTSD. Research suggests that some people are at greater risk for developing PTSD after a trauma. The risk of PTSD is higher for those with a history of being abused as a child, poor social support, low socioeconomic status, personal and family history of psychiatric problems, and among women. Some ethnic groups are more likely than others to develop PTSD, even after taking demographic variables and traumatic exposure into account. For example, in the United States, African Americans, Latinos, and Native Americans are more likely to develop PTSD than non-Latino whites, while Asian Americans are less likely to develop PTSD than non-Latino whites.

Certain types of incidents and experiences are more likely than others to result in PTSD. For example, PTSD is more likely to develop after a trauma that involves intentional harm (e.g., sexual assault) versus a trauma that was not intentional (e.g., a tornado). Although women are about ten times more likely than men to be the victims of rape, men are more liable to develop PTSD after being raped than are women (65% of men and 46%

of women). Men, on the other hand, are much less likely to develop PTSD after a physical assault (1.8% of men and 21.3% of women).

OBSESSIVE-COMPULSIVE DISORDER

Obsessive-compulsive disorder (OCD) is characterized by _obsessions_ (reoccurring, uncontrollable, unwanted thoughts, images, or urges) and _compulsions_ (repetitive behaviors or mental acts that the individuals feels he or she must complete in response to the obsession). Compulsive behaviors may be observable to others, but they may also involve mental rituals (e.g., counting, silent prayers, mentally checking to make sure that one is not sick) that others cannot perceive.

To use a typical example, an individual with OCD related to cleanliness might touch the doorknob at a public restroom, which would trigger the obsessive thought "I'm going to get sick." This cognition, in turn, might lead him or her to engage in compulsive handwashing to neutralize the obsessive thought. Although the compulsive behavior in OCD arises in response to the obsession, there is either no realistic connection between the compulsion and the obsessive fear (e.g., someone avoids writing the number "13" due to fear that he will die if he writes these numbers), or the compulsion is an excessive reaction to the obsession (e.g., someone who fears burning down her home repeatedly checks to make sure the stove is turned off). (See Table 2 for examples of obsessions and associated compulsions).

OCD is diagnosed only if the obsessions or compulsions are time-consuming (defined by the _DSM-5_ as taking more than one hour per day), cause impairment in functioning, or cause significant distress. It is interesting to note that it has become common for those who like to be neat and tidy, or for those who prefer to keep their desks organized, to describe themselves by saying "I'm so OCD." In such cases, this phrase is used to indicate a quirky preference for neatness. In contrast to this depiction of OCD, individuals who have diagnosable OCD often struggle to cope with the demands of life and feel tormented by their thoughts. In fact, recent research suggests that those with OCD are ten times more likely to commit suicide than those in the general population.

Those with OCD often have dysfunctional beliefs that increase their distress. These beliefs can include perfectionism, an inflated sense of responsibility, and _thought-action fusion_, which refers to the belief that simply thinking about an action is equivalent to performing the action. Individuals with OCD vary regarding their level of insight into the dysfunctional nature of their beliefs. At the healthier end of the spectrum, a person with _good or fair_ insight might wash his or her hands for several hours per day,

Table 2 Categories of OCD and Examples of Associated Obsessions and Compulsions

Category	Obsession	Compulsion
Aggressive	Fear of acting on an impulse to harm a family member	Avoidance of looking at kitchen knives when family members are present
Contamination	Worry about contracting an illness after touching a doorknob	Excessive handwashing
Sexual	Concern about whether one is attracted to members of the same sex	Watching pornography involving members of one's sex while scanning body for signs of arousal or disgust
Hoarding/ saving	Worry about throwing away objects due to irrational fear that they may be needed in the future	Saving objects, such as bottles or candy wrappers, that have no monetary or sentimental value and no practical use
Religious	Fear of having violated morality by withholding the "truth" about oneself from others	Needing to confess all "bad" thoughts or behaviors to friends or family members
Symmetry or exactness	Perfectionistic need for handwritten words to look "right"	Repeatedly erasing and rewriting the same letter, word, or sentence until satisfied
Miscellaneous	Worry that certain numbers are bad luck	Tapping leg a certain number of times to counteract the effects of the "bad number"
Somatic	Excessive worry— despite reassurance by others—that one's nose is hideously unattractive	Looking at oneself in the mirror for several hours per day while focusing on this perceived negative feature

Source: Adapted from Goodman, W.K., Price, L.H., Rasmussen, S.A., Mazure, C., Fleischmann, R.L., Hill, C.L., et al. (1989a). The Yale-Brown Obsessive Compulsive Scale. I. Development, use, and reliability. *Archives of General Psychiatry,* 46, 1006–1011.

but would be aware that he or she is unlikely to contract AIDS from touching a doorknob. At the more severe end of the spectrum, someone with *absent insight* or *delusional beliefs* (4% or less of those with OCD) would fully believe that contact with a doorknob will lead to an AIDS infection.

According to the DSM-5, the median age of onset for OCD in the United States is 19.5 years. While females are slightly more likely to develop OCD in adulthood, males tend to have an earlier age of onset, with 25 percent of males having an onset before age ten. The 12-month prevalence of OCD among adults in the United States is 1.2 percent, and its prevalence is similar in other countries. If untreated, the course of OCD is usually chronic, and symptoms tend to wax and wane over the lifetime. Research suggests that, from the time that their symptoms first emerge, it takes an average of ten years for people with OCD to get into treatment.

While there is no single identifiable cause for OCD, research that suggests that in some children, OCD can be triggered or exacerbated by a streptococcal infection. Children who experience a sudden onset or worsening of OCD symptoms or tics following such infections are diagnosed with pediatric autoimmune neuropsychiatric disorders associated with streptococcal infections, or PANDAS. Experts believe that in its attempts to fight the strep molecules, the immune system inadvertently also attacks some of its own cells. The resulting damage to these cells leads to OCD, tics, and other symptoms observed in those with PANDAS. Experts generally agree that children with PANDAS should be treated using the same medications and psychotherapy that are provided to those who have more typical OCD.

9. How common are anxiety disorders? Who tends to get them?

Answers to these questions come from the field of epidemiology, which is a branch of science that studies patterns of illness in a population. Research on the epidemiology of anxiety disorders became much more common after the publication of the DSM-III in 1980, which for the first time laid out specific criteria for psychiatric disorders, allowing researchers to develop questionnaires that could reliably be used in studies across the world. With the wide adoption of the DSM criteria, researchers were able to investigate the prevalence of anxiety disorders (i.e., how many people in a population have a condition), the age at which the disorder typically appears, and the course an illness is likely to follow across the lifespan.

PREVALENCE RATES

Researchers sometimes seek to determine what percentage of a population currently has a condition (*point prevalence*), what proportion has had an illness in the past year (*12-month prevalence*), or what percentage has had a condition at any point in their lives (*lifetime prevalence*). It should be noted that the prevalence figures reviewed later in the chapter offer an estimate of how many people in a given population could be diagnosed with an anxiety disorder based on their responses to survey questions. The prevalence estimates do not tell us how many people have actually been diagnosed with an anxiety disorder, but it is a safe assumption that far fewer people are diagnosed or treated than the number of people who could be diagnosed based on *DSM* criteria.

With this caveat in mind, epidemiological research has shown that anxiety and related disorders (a group that includes obsessive-compulsive disorder [OCD] and post-traumatic stress disorder [PTSD]) are the most common psychiatric illnesses in the United States and across the world. In the United States, the National Institute of Mental Health (NIMH) estimates that over the course of a 12-month period, 18.1 percent of adults in the United States—40 million people—have an anxiety disorder. Among those adults with an anxiety disorder, NIMH estimates that one-quarter of these individuals, or around 10 million adults in the United States, have anxiety that is considered "severe." Ronald Kessler, a leading researcher in the epidemiology of mental health, found that over the course of their lifetimes, 28.8 percent of the U.S. population has had an anxiety disorder. Furthermore, NIMH has found that 25.1 percent of adolescents have qualified for an anxiety disorder diagnosis at some time between the ages of 13 and 18 (30.1% of females and 20.3% of males).

Anxiety disorders are more prevalent in some demographic groups than in others. Among adults in the United States, women are 60 percent more likely than men to develop an anxiety disorder over the course of their lifetimes. Prevalence rates in the United States also vary across different racial and ethnic groups; the lifetime prevalence of anxiety disorders among non-Hispanic whites is 30 percent higher than for Hispanics and 20 percent higher than for non-Hispanic blacks.

Looking at prevalence rates across the world, a recent meta-analysis (meaning a study that combines data from other studies) reviewed 34 years' worth of data collected in 63 countries. These researchers found that over the course of a 12-month period, 6.7 percent of adults world-wide had an anxiety disorder. Women were roughly twice as likely as men to have had an anxiety disorder over the previous 12 months (8.7% vs. 4.3%). Over the course of a lifetime, 12.9 percent of adults had experienced an anxiety disorder. There is significant geographic variation in the prevalence of anxiety disorders. One survey found that anxiety disorders had a lifetime prevalence rate of 31 percent in the United States, which was the highest in the world, whereas the lifetime prevalence in China was 4.8 percent, which was the world's lowest.

Epidemiological research indicates that although anxiety disorders appear to exist across all cultures, some conditions are more common in certain parts of the world. Studies have found that 6 to 12 percent of people have had a specific phobia at some point in their lives, making this the world's most common anxiety disorder. The next most prevalent disorder is social anxiety disorder, which affects about 10 percent of people across their lifetimes. Social anxiety disorder is more common in North America than in Western Europe. In Japan, there is a variant of social phobia called taijin kyofusho. In contrast to the form of social anxiety seen in other parts of the world, in which the sufferer fears being embarrassed himself or herself, taijin sufferers fear embarrassing others. Interestingly, unlike other anxiety disorders, taijin kyofusho is more common among men than women.

The third most common disorder involving anxiety is PTSD, which is more common in countries whose residents have greater exposure to trauma. For example, in the United States, which has high levels of interpersonal violence, PTSD has a lifetime prevalence of about 9 percent. In Western Europe, which has significantly lower levels of interpersonal violence, the lifetime prevalence of PTSD is 1 to 2 percent. The highest levels of PTSD are seen in countries with ongoing sectarian violence, such as Israel, Nigeria, and South Africa, where the lifetime prevalence of PTSD is estimated to be over 10 percent. Worldwide lifetime prevalence estimates for GAD range between 3 and 5 percent, between 2 and 5 percent for panic disorder, between 2 and 3 percent for OCD and separation anxiety disorder, and around 2 percent for agoraphobia without panic disorder. Among children and adolescents (generally defined as those up to age 19), the most common anxiety disorders, in order, are specific phobia, social anxiety disorder, and separation anxiety disorder. Selective mutism is a rare condition, and it appears in 0.7 to 0.8 percent of children and adolescents.

Interestingly, anxiety disorders seem to be more common in recent generations. Research has found that over the course of their lifetimes, those born in the 1990s are more likely to develop an anxiety disorder than those born in the 1940s. There is a great deal of controversy surrounding the observed increase in prevalence; some argue that it reflects a genuine increase in the prevalence of anxiety disorders across generations, while others say that the differences are due to methodological issues.

AGE OF ONSET

Epidemiologists have gathered information on the age of onset for anxiety disorders (i.e., the age at which people develop the condition). Researchers have found that anxiety disorders, which have a median age of onset of 11, tend to start earlier in life than other common psychiatric disorders, including substance use disorders (median age 20) or mood disorders (median age 30).

Within the category of anxiety disorders, the various conditions show different age-of-onset patterns. Specific phobias tend to start the earliest: among all people who develop a specific phobia over their lifetimes, the majority will do so before the age of 18. OCD and social anxiety disorder tend to have their onset during adolescence or young adulthood, and most people with these conditions have developed them by their 20s. GAD, panic disorder, and agoraphobia tend to develop later in life, and there is more variability in their ages of onset than specific phobias, social phobia, or OCD. Among anxiety and related disorders, PTSD tends to have the latest age of onset as well as the greatest variability in when it develops. This is likely because people can be exposed to trauma at any point in life.

Despite the early age of onset for anxiety disorders relative to other psychiatric disorders, people with anxiety disorders do not typically receive treatment until adulthood, which is often many years after the disorder first appeared. Some researchers, noting that people with early-onset anxiety disorders are at increased risk for developing substance abuse problems and other forms of mental illness, have argued that more resources should be allocated to diagnosing and treating childhood anxiety. The hope is that treating anxiety in childhood will reduce an individual's risk of developing another disorder in the future, but this hypothesis, although reasonable, has not been tested empirically.

COURSE OF ILLNESS

Researchers looking at the course of illness are trying to learn how a condition typically "behaves" over time. For example, the course of illness for amyotrophic lateral sclerosis (ALS), otherwise known as Lou Gehrig's disease, is progressive and follows a predictable sequence ending in death. Prostate cancer, on the other hand, has a much less predictable course, as some tumors grow very slowly and never cause any noticeable problems, while more aggressive cancers can prove fatal in a matter of months.

Researchers have learned that when untreated, anxiety disorders tend to follow a chronic course, meaning that although the severity of symptoms waxes and wanes over time, these conditions typically last for many years. One study found that among the disorders they included, those with social phobia were least likely to recover over a 12-year period (37%), while those who had panic disorder without agoraphobia were most likely to recover (82%).

Unfortunately, those who do recover often find that their anxiety disorders return at a later date. Depending on the specific condition, the number of people who recover from anxiety and then have their anxiety disorders recur ranges from 39 to 58 percent. People were about half as likely to recover from an anxiety disorder if they also had depression. Those who did recover were around twice as likely to have their anxiety disorders return if they also had depression.

10. Why are women more likely than men to be diagnosed with an anxiety disorder?

Both in the United States and globally, women are significantly more likely than men to develop an anxiety disorder over the course of their lives. This is true for anxiety disorders as a generic category, and many studies have found this to be true for each anxiety disorder. This divergence in the incidence of anxiety disorders seems to start at around age six, and it continues through adolescence and adulthood. How do scientists explain these findings?

To answer this question, we will review some of the mechanisms that have been researched, including biology, stress- and trauma-related factors, cognitive factors, behavioral factors, and cultural factors. This topic is still under debate, but it is clear that the gender disparity in anxiety disorders is not reducible to a single cause.

BIOLOGY: HORMONAL

If the rates of anxiety between men and women were different only in the United States, then it would be reasonable to assume that the disparity is caused purely by culture. However, the fact that this pattern has been observed across the world has led researchers to suggest a biological basis for these differences. In support of this idea, researchers have found that women are more likely to experience anxiety, depression, and other mood symptoms during periods of hormonal change, such as puberty, the premenstrual period, during pregnancy, after giving birth, and during menopause.

Furthermore, research suggests that men's higher testosterone levels may have a protective effect against anxiety and depression. Evidence for this hypothesis comes from several sources, including research on men with hypogonadism, a condition that leads to decreased testosterone production. Men with this condition are more likely to have anxiety and depression, but this tendency is no longer seen in men with hypogonadism who receive testosterone replacement therapy. The beneficial effect of testosterone on anxiety and depression has also been observed in women, as researchers have found that the administration of a low dose of testosterone led to improvements in women who had treatment-resistant depression. Though low doses of testosterone may be helpful to some women, researchers have cautioned that higher doses can lead to worsening mood and may trigger a depressive episode.

EXPERIENCE: STRESS AND TRAUMA

While experts once thought that women had higher rates of post-traumatic stress disorder (PTSD) due to experiencing more potentially traumatic events (PTEs) in their lives, recent research suggests that this is true only for certain types of PTEs. Men, it turns out, are more likely than women to experience nonsexual assaults, combat/war, accidents, witnessing death or injury, and disasters (e.g., fire or tornado). Women are more likely than men, however, to experience attempted rape, rape, and domestic abuse. Young girls are also more likely than boys to be the victims of child sexual abuse, which is associated with the later development of many different psychiatric illnesses.

COGNITIVE: THREAT APPRAISAL

It is theorized that women are more likely than men to overestimate the probability of danger, to view the world as unpredictable and overwhelming, and to anticipate harm. Beginning in childhood, girls are also better than boys at detecting others' emotions based on facial expressions and other nonverbal cues. This makes girls more aware that a caregiver is feeling anxious or afraid, thereby increasing the likelihood that they will learn that their environment is dangerous. These factors may partially explain the greater incidence of anxiety disorders among girls and women, as they are more likely than males to experience the world around them as dangerous and hostile, thus priming more girls and women to make the transition from experiencing a potentially traumatic event to developing PTSD or another anxiety disorder.

CULTURAL: GENDER ROLE SOCIALIZATION

Sandra Bem's gender role theory suggests that societies communicate to children which behaviors are acceptable for their gender, rewarding those who embody these norms, and punishing those who do not. In this view, boys are taught to be tough, to avoid expressing emotion, and to be assertive, whereas girls are taught to be meek, emotionally expressive, and avoidant of conflict. In such a social context, expressions of fear are more closely associated with high levels of femininity and low levels of masculinity.

As an example, when a boy scrapes his knee and cries, his parents may tell him to get up and keep playing, which communicates to him that he is competent and resilient. If a girl falls and scrapes her knee, her parents might pick her up and hug her for several minutes, kiss her knee until she stops crying, and encourage her to run slower next time. This communicates to girls that they should avoid risk and that they must be protected and soothed by others. Through many repetitions of such interactions, boys and girls are taught different ways of coping that influence their beliefs about how threatening the world is, how capable they are of tolerating and overcoming distress, and the extent to which they should rely on others to help them manage difficulties.

Gender role norms may also explain why men are less likely than women to seek help for anxiety and depression. From a young age, boys are told to "suck it up" and deal with problems by themselves. By contrast, girls are taught to express positive emotion through affection and sadness through crying and are also taught that it's acceptable to ask for help from others when they feel the need.

BEHAVIORAL: SUBSTANCE USE

Researchers have found that men and women respond differently to stress and that whereas women tend to react with sadness or anxiety, men are more likely to drink alcohol or use substances in response to stress. Indeed, while women are more likely than men to have an anxiety disorder or depression, men are more likely than women to have problems with alcoholism and have a higher likelihood of being diagnosed with a substance abuse disorder. Interestingly, though men are more likely than women to abuse marijuana and alcohol, women are more likely than men to become addicted to sedatives and antianxiety medications, perhaps reflecting the higher intensity of anxiety experienced by women. While there are biological differences in the ways that men and women respond to substances, it remains unclear to what extent the differences in substance use are biological versus environmental.

Causes and Risk Factors

11. Why do some people develop anxiety disorders?

When people search for the causes of an individual's anxiety disorder, there is a natural tendency to look for simple answers. Why is John so scared of dogs? He was bitten as a child. Why does Rowen get panic attacks? There is a chemical imbalance in her brain. Why does Naizer cry for hours when his parents drop him off at school? His parents must not take good care of him at home. Why do Tiffany, her sister, and her mother all have to take medication for anxiety? It must be some genetic problem.

This was the approach taken by early theorists, whose explanations for the etiology of anxiety disorders rested exclusively on either biology (i.e., nature) or environment (i.e., nurture). There is now convincing evidence that anxiety disorders have no single cause and are generated by a complex interaction of many different factors, which include genetics, neuroanatomy, information processing, and life experiences. For example, although certain parental behaviors have been linked to the development of anxiety disorders in their children, experts recognize that parental influences are only one link in a much larger chain of external events and internal processes that can eventually culminate in an anxiety disorder.

The concepts of multifinality and equifinality offer a useful way to think about the complex interactions that give rise to anxiety disorders.

The principle of *equifinality* explains that many pathways can lead to the same destination, meaning that, for example, many different combinations of genetic vulnerabilities and environmental stresses can result in the eventual development of panic disorder. *Multifinality* describes the way in which a single pathway, such as childhood trauma, can result in several different outcomes, including post-traumatic stress disorder, phobias, and panic disorder.

Rather than searching for causes, researchers think more in terms of risk factors for the development of anxiety disorders. Unlike causes, which must always be present for an effect to be observed, risk factors are variables that are associated with an increased likelihood of a given illness. For example, AIDS is always *caused* by HIV, since a person must first have been infected with HIV to develop AIDS. By contrast, smoking is considered a *risk factor* for lung cancer, since people may not develop this condition even though they smoke, and others get cancer without ever having smoked a cigarette. People develop anxiety disorders when they have biological and psychological risk factors that make them more vulnerable to stress and when they live in an environment that pushes them to their breaking point. In short, biological and psychological risk factors load the gun, and environmental events pull the trigger.

An exhaustive review of the risk factors for anxiety disorders is beyond the scope of this book, but some of the most critical risk factors are reviewed in this chapter.

BIOLOGICAL FACTORS

Due to innate physiology, some people are born with greater vulnerability to anxiety. High levels of maternal stress during pregnancy are correlated with higher anxiety in the child at age four, perhaps due to the damaging effects of cortisol, a stress hormone, on developing brain structures while *in utero*. Being born female is one of the most significant biological risk factors for anxiety disorders. By age six, girls are about twice as likely as boys to develop anxiety disorders, and this pattern continues through adolescence and adulthood. (See Question 10 titled "Why are women more likely than men to be diagnosed with an anxiety disorder?" for more information on the relationship between gender and anxiety.)

Temperament, which refers to biologically based behavioral patterns of behavior and character traits that are stable across multiple contexts in early development, provides one of the earliest signs that a child is vulnerable to developing an anxiety disorder. Infants with a temperamental style characterized by "behavioral inhibition" have a greater tendency to withdraw from novel stimuli and show heightened physio-logical reactivity to unfamiliar situations. Infants judged as behaviorally inhibited are at an increased risk for social anxiety disorder. Some children naturally "grow out" of behavioral inhibition, but those children whose inhibition remains stable are at greater risk for anxiety disorders across their lifetimes.

Based on multiple lines of research, scientists have concluded that an individual's likelihood of developing an anxiety disorder is strongly related to his or her genes. Researchers have demonstrated that children who have a first-degree relative with an anxiety disorder are significantly more likely to develop an anxiety disorder than those without anxiety-disordered relatives. Twin studies, which compare the rates of anxiety disorders among monozygotic versus dizygotic twins (i.e., identical versus fraternal), lend additional weight to the assertion that genetics play an important role in anxiety disorders. (See Question 13 titled "Can anxiety be inherited?" for more information on the genetics of anxiety disorders.)

There is some evidence that the presence or absence of certain genes can affect human behavior. Researchers found that variations in a gene called *RGS2*, which modulates norepinephrine and serotonin receptors in the brain, are associated with behaviorally inhibited temperament. Another study found that after a severe hurricane season in Florida, those with a certain variant of the *RGS2* gene were more likely to have developed an anxiety disorder. Research in this area does not prove that variations in the *RGS2* gene directly cause anxiety disorders, but these studies do suggest that differences in particular genes can alter the functioning of fear systems and can make people more vulnerable to anxiety, which may, in turn, increase their risk of developing a disorder.

ENVIRONMENTAL FACTORS

Anxiety disorders are more common among those with lower socioeconomic status, and for unknown reasons, prevalence also seems to vary by ethnicity. For example, researchers have found that Caucasian children tended to report higher social anxiety, while African American children were more likely to report separation anxiety. It is possible, albeit unlikely, that particular ethnicities have a biological predisposition toward specific anxiety disorders, and it seems probable that variations in prevalence are due to cultural influences or differential exposure to stressors. Though anxiety disorders appear to exist in all cultures, an individual's cultural context seems to determine the way in which the anxiety will be expressed and the subjective meaning of the experience. Some cultures, for example, have specific beliefs about the functioning of the body or about supernatural forces that shape the expression of anxiety. (See Question 30 titled "How does culture impact anxiety?" for more information on this topic.)

Beyond the influence of genetics, some maladaptive patterns of interaction between parents and children (reviewed in Question 12 titled "How does parenting affect anxiety?") can contribute to the development of anxiety disorders. Some aspects of the family environment, such as frequent hostile conflict between parents, low levels of emotional support, low emotional expressiveness, are associated with anxiety disorders in children. The loss of a parent before age 17 (due to death or separation lasting over a year) is a risk factor for generalized anxiety disorder, phobias, and panic disorder in adulthood. Furthermore, children who were subjected to physical abuse, emotional abuse, sexual abuse, and neglect are at a substantially increased risk of having anxiety disorders (and for depression) in adulthood. Childhood trauma was also associated with the presence of comorbid conditions and with more chronic mental illness.

PSYCHOLOGICAL FACTORS

Cognitive models emphasize the role of unhelpful and inaccurate thoughts in generating and maintaining anxiety disorders, while behavioral models focus more heavily on the role of classical and operant conditioning. (Note: because the behavioral model is discussed extensively in Question 14 titled "How do people develop irrational fears of spiders, dogs, heights, and so on?" this discussion will focus on cognitive explanations.) Cognitive vulnerabilities to anxiety include heightened vigilance, a tendency to pay greater attention to threat-relevant information, and biases in judgment that cause people to overestimate the likelihood of negative events.

Anxiety sensitivity, which is a fear of anxious physical sensations due to a belief that the sensations will cause physical, psychological, or social harm, is higher in those with most anxiety disorders than those without. Anxiety sensitivity is thought to play an especially important role in panic disorder. Consistent with the concept of anxiety sensitivity, David Clark suggested that some people are at an elevated risk for ongoing panic attacks because they (1) have a heightened sensitivity to bodily sensations and (2) because, noticing these changes, they make catastrophic interpretations of these feelings. Someone without panic disorder, for example, might lose their breath as they walk up a flight of stairs, but this momentary discomfort would not cause distress. In contrast, someone with panic disorder is likely to be hyper-aware of their breathing difficulties and to misinterpret the experience as a sign that they are going to lose consciousness or have a heart attack.

Anxiety sensitivity and misinterpretation of one's experiences are thought to play an especially important role in panic disorder, but they are also relevant to other anxiety disorders. People with social anxiety disorder tend to fear anxiety-related sensations because they worry that sweating, trembling, or difficulty speaking will result in social rejection. Test anxiety has been linked to excessive focus on one's thoughts and physical sensations, which detract from test performance.

Like the misinterpretations of physical sensations seen in anxiety sensitivity, cognitive theories suggest that the obsessions in obsessive-compulsive disorder (OCD) are caused by a tendency to misinterpret the significance of one's thoughts. Everyone occasionally experiences thoughts or images that he or she finds horrifying or repugnant. If someone believes that these unwanted thoughts reveal something important about who one truly is, the thoughts are likely to elicit distress. When people attempt to suppress these cognitions, the thoughts tend to multiply instead. Ongoing attempts to avoid these distressing thoughts and images eventually result in compulsive rituals, at which point OCD has begun to take form.

In many ways, research on risk factors for anxiety is similar to the parable of the blind men and the elephant. With each man touching a different part of the elephant, they are in complete disagreement about the attributes of the animal, since each man can only describe the small section they are touching. Similarly, researchers looking at the etiology of anxiety disorders typically approach the topic from the perspective of a particular discipline, such as genetics, parenting, or neurobiology. While each of these areas has offered important contributions to the field, none provides a complete explanation for why one individual develops an anxiety disorder while another does not.

In the questions that follow, we will examine some of the factors that are associated with the development of anxiety disorders.

12. How does parenting affect anxiety?

The parent–child relationship is thought to influence the development of anxiety in three ways: (1) through rejection and/or overprotectiveness;

(2) through modeling by the parent, which teaches the child how to respond to anxiety-provoking situations and teaches the child what is and is not safe; and (3) through the security/insecurity of the attachment relationship. Given the importance of attachment theory to many areas of psychology and human development, we will focus our attention mainly on this line of inquiry.

REJECTION AND OVERPROTECTIVENESS

Researchers have identified two dimensions of parental styles, acceptance/support versus rejection, and granting of autonomy versus control, which impact the developing child's predisposition toward anxiety. Parental rejection refers to disapproval, low responsiveness and attention, coldness, and criticalness. Parental control relates to setting excessive rules that limit the child's autonomy. These patterns of parental behavior are theorized to increase anxiety by communicating that the world is unsafe, that the child will not be supported, and that the child is not competent to successfully navigate life.

MODELING

Researchers have demonstrated that children learn from their parents how to respond to anxiety-provoking situations. Parental behaviors that teach or reinforce fearful responses are a risk factor for the development of anxiety disorders in children. This learning can happen in several ways. In the form of teaching known as "modeling," children may observe their parents' fearful responses and imitate their behavior (e.g., the child sees his or her father recoil in fear from a dog and then does the same). The child can learn through verbal statements made by parents that communicate danger (e.g., "Tommy, stay away from that dog because you never know when he'll attack"). Finally, parents can increase a child's fear by reinforcing avoidance (e.g., the father drives the son to school, so the son doesn't have to walk past a house with a barking dog).

ATTACHMENT

John Bowlby, a British psychoanalyst who was trained by one of Freud's protégés, was the first to advance the idea that a person's relationship with early attachment figures (generally the mother) largely determines his or her level of anxiety and the health of later relationships. Attachment theory, as it later became known, suggests that an infant has a biological need to develop a relationship with a primary caregiver to ensure his or her survival. Bowlby theorized that a healthy early relationship with a caregiver provided a secure base from which the infant could explore its environment. This secure relationship helped the child to develop an "internal working model" of maternal love and security that provided a template for healthy relationships in childhood, adolescence, and adulthood. By contrast, those mother–infant relationships that Bowlby characterized as "insecure"—in which the mother was seen as distant, inconsistent, or smothering—led infants to be less willing to explore their environments and to behave in a way that indicated anxiety and agitation. Such babies, Bowlby suggested, tended to go on to become more anxious and inhibited, to have poorer relationships, and to be less capable of navigating the demands of life.

Through her pioneering research using the Strange Situation procedure, Mary Ainsworth helped Bowlby to expand on his theory and described additional categories of attachment relationships. In the Strange Situation, infants between 12 and 20 months are observed in a laboratory setting as they react to caregivers and strangers entering and leaving the room. As a partial description of the Strange Situation, an infant would first play in the room with only his mother present, and then after a minute, a stranger would enter the room and try to interact with the child, after which the child's mother would leave the room for three minutes while the stranger remained. The mother would then return, and infants were then classified as having one of three "attachment styles" (with a fourth category later added) based on their behavioral response to being alone with a stranger and then reunited with their mothers.

"Securely attached" children could interact with the stranger while their mothers were present, were distressed when their parents left, and were quickly soothed after they returned. The mothers of these infants tended to be affectionate, attentive, and responsive to their child's displays of emotion. Infants labeled as having "ambivalent attachment" would become extremely distressed when their mothers left the room and would respond to their mother's return by clinging to them and hitting them. The mothers of these infants tended to be inconsistent in their responses; at times, they were sensitive to their child's needs, while at other times they showed little interest or response to their children. Babies categorized as having "avoidant attachment" showed little distress in response to their mother's absence and had minimal response to their return. Their mothers tended to be distant and disengaged. Infants categorized as having "disorganized attachment" would respond to the Strange Situation in ways that demonstrated no clear way of coping, as indicated by freezing in place, by seeming dazed or disoriented, or by responding atypically (e.g., by hiding when their mothers returned). Mothers of infants in this category were described as responding in ways that were "frightened and frightening," unpredictable, and either passive or intrusive.

In the decades since Ainsworth published her initial work on the Strange Situation, researchers have attempted to determine whether attachment styles in infancy had a longer-term impact on an individual's development. One of the most well known of these research projects, the Minnesota Study of Risk and Adaptation from Birth to Adulthood, has been following the same group of people since the mid-1970s. Participants in this study were assessed at 12 months and 18 months old using the Strange Situation to classify their attachment styles. In 2005, results based on 30 years of data showed that when compared to their securely attached peers, the infants with ambivalent and avoidant attachment styles were more dependent on teachers in elementary and middle school, had poorer social skills as adolescents, and had less positive romantic relationships as adults. In comparison to infants with avoidant or secure attachment styles, those who had been classified as having an ambivalent attachment style as infants were more likely to develop problems with anxiety by the age of 17. A disorganized attachment style in infancy predicted greater impulse control problems, an increased tendency toward dissociation, and a higher risk of developing conduct disorder (which can be thought of as the adolescent version of antisocial personality disorder).

It may seem unjust that those who have had the misfortune to develop an ambivalent attachment style as infants should also have to struggle with greater anxiety throughout the lifespan. However, this may actually offer an evolutionary advantage, as increased anxiety may allow these individuals to be more vigilant to threats. Given that they have received less consistent support from their caregivers, this may enable them to cope more effectively with a world that is realistically more dangerous for them than it is for their securely attached peers, who are more likely to be able to rely on caregivers in times of stress. Interestingly, researchers studying the offspring of Holocaust survivors have found that their children and grandchildren show elevated levels of stress hormones and more intense behavioral and physiological reactivity to stressful images than ethnically similar offspring of those who were not exposed to the Holocaust. Having endured this trauma, it is as though the survivors are communicating to their descendants that they must be vigilant against future threats.

13. Can anxiety be inherited?

Made up of a segment of deoxyribonucleic acid (DNA), a gene is a set of instructions that tells a cell what to do. People have two copies of every gene, one of which comes from each parent. About 99.9 percent of DNA is the same in all people, but variations in just 0.1 percent of these instructions give rise to many of the differences between individuals. Heritability describes the degree to which variation for a given trait can be attributed to genetic differences versus environmental factors. Some features, like eye color and blood type, are entirely heritable and are not influenced by the environment. Other traits, like a preference for a particular style of music, are completely acquired (or learned) and are not affected by heredity. Still others, like height, are influenced by both genetics and environment. Given this information, are anxiety disorders coded into our genes, or are they caused by the environment?

Though there is some disagreement about the relative influence of "nature" versus "nurture," it is now widely accepted that both environment and genes play a role in the development of anxiety disorders. Many studies have shown that people who have a first-degree relative with an anxiety disorder are 4–6 times more likely to develop the same anxiety disorder than those without affected family members. Compared to other anxiety-related conditions, panic disorder is most likely to be shared by family members. One study found that those with a first-degree relative with panic disorder were ten times more likely to this condition than those without panic-disordered family members.

Furthermore, the results of a study on 10,000 people suggest that with each additional family member who has an anxiety disorder, a child's risk of developing an anxiety disorder gets progressively higher. The survey results showed that a child had a 10 percent chance of developing an anxiety disorder if he or she had no relatives with such a condition, a 30 percent chance if one family member had an anxiety disorder, and a 70 percent chance if a majority of family members had an anxiety disorder. This phenomenon is known among researchers as "familial aggregation due to genetic risk."

The fact that anxiety disorders aggregate in families does not prove that anxiety is genetic because family members share the same environment as well as genes. To separate the effects of nature and nurture, researchers compare the rates of a given disorder among sets of twins. You may recall that fraternal twins share 50 percent of their genes, which is the same amount shared by any biological sibling, whereas identical twins share (roughly) 100 percent of their DNA. When identical twins differ on any trait, such as athleticism, height, or intelligence, these differences must have been caused by environmental variables that were experienced by only one twin.

By comparing the similarity of identical twins versus fraternal twins, these studies provide evidence of the degree to which a trait or condition is genetically determined. If, for example, IQ scores are more similar among identical twins than fraternal twins, then this greater similarity in intelligence can be attributed to their genetic similarity. If the IQ scores of identical twins are no more similar than those observed among fraternal twins, this would indicate that IQ is more heavily influenced by the environment. Twin studies on anxiety disorders have estimated that these conditions are 20–40 percent heritable. These estimates suggest that the heritability of anxiety disorders is roughly on par with depression, but that they are significantly less heritable than schizophrenia and bipolar disorder.

Though twin studies indicate that anxiety disorders have a genetic component, they don't tell us which specific genes are involved. Unfortunately, locating the genes that lead to anxiety disorders has been more difficult than scientists hoped. Some medical disorders, such as Huntington disease, are caused by mutations in a single gene, meaning that those who have this faulty gene are basically guaranteed to develop the condition. Anxiety disorders, in contrast, are considered "complex disorders" because they are influenced by many genetic risk factors. Individually, each risk factor has a small effect, and they may lead to a disorder only when the person experiences sustained high stress or a significant trauma.

Despite these difficulties, scientists have identified several genes that may be involved. This has been accomplished by comparing the DNA of those with a disorder against those without the illness, or by analyzing the DNA of families in which several members have anxiety disorders. Perhaps more interestingly, using a technique that allows them to turn mouse genes on and off, scientists have tested how particular genes influence defensive responses. Eric Kandel, a Nobel Prize–winning neuroscientist, identified a gene called *stathmin* that appears to be required for fear learning in mice. Unlike most mice, which avoid open spaces and prefer to hide in corners, mice whose *stathmin* gene was shut off were much more adventurous. Such mice ventured into open areas with no apparent fear of potential dangers. Furthermore, normal mice quickly learn to associate a particular tone with an electric shock. After a few pairings of the sound and shock, normal mice freeze in anticipation of the shock as soon as they hear the tone. Mice without *stathmin*, however, continued to go about their normal activities when presented with this sound, seemingly unafraid of the coming shock. Of course, it is not possible to do similar research on humans, but scientists hope that these findings can tell us something about how anxiety and fear work in other species, which could eventually translate into more effective treatments for humans.

14. How do people develop irrational fears of spiders, dogs, heights, and so on?

While many people would probably prefer not to find a spider crawling on their arm, some people respond with extreme fear to seeing a spider on the other side of a room. Other individuals may close their eyes to avoid seeing movie scenes that involve snakes, get uncomfortably sweaty and distressed at the mere mention of public speaking, or hide behind their children in fear when a friendly chihuahua comes into view. Such individuals may qualify for a diagnosis of specific phobia, which is a persistent and intense fear of a particular situation or object that is disproportionate to the actual threat. To those who do not have such a fear, the response of phobic individuals may seem so over-the-top that it can appear comical. *How*, the observer may wonder, *can someone be so scared of something so harmless? Do they really think that small puppy is going to hurt them when it's on a leash and 20 feet away?* The answer is that people who suffer from phobias are often aware that their fears are irrational, and yet they may still feel powerless to change their emotional reaction. If this is the case, how do these fears develop? More broadly, how do we learn which things to fear?

Before answering this question, it is important to acknowledge that there is evidence that genetics have a strong influence on an individual's propensity to develop phobias. Furthermore, research suggests that humans have been programmed by natural selection to more readily acquire some fears as opposed to others. It is probably obvious that certain objects and situations are much more likely to elicit fear than others. One would not be surprised, for example, to learn that a new acquaintance was afraid of heights, but would probably be quite surprised if the person was terrified of marshmallows. Certain fears, which are easily learned, difficult to extinguish, and common in phobias, are sometimes referred to as "prepared fears," meaning that humans are biologically prepared to acquire these fears.

Through much of our evolutionary history, humans have been under threat by animals (e.g., snakes, spiders, and large carnivores), infectious disease, and social exclusion—all of which could have resulted in death. Our forebears who learned to avoid these dangers were more likely to survive long enough to pass their genes on to subsequent generations. Over many thousands of years, the propensity to develop fears of these stimuli made its way into our genes.

Because technological progress moves at a far faster pace than evolution, modern humans have not been able to recalibrate their fear responses to match the dangers of their current environment. To illustrate this point, consider the following statistics from the Centers for Disease Control and Prevention: every year in the United States, heart disease is responsible for 610,000 deaths, whereas five people per year die from snake bites. Americans are therefore 122,000 times more likely to be killed by cardiac problems than from a snake bite. While many people are highly fearful of snakes, the popularity of fast food suggests that a fear of cheeseburgers is far less common.

Researchers focusing on the contribution of the environment to the development of phobias have speculated that people can develop fears through "associative learning," in which an individual learns that different events, behaviors, or stimuli are connected to one another. If someone develops a fear of dogs after being bitten, they have learned that a stimulus (dog) is associated with an aversive outcome (pain). The association of "dog" and "pain" can be learned through direct traumatic experience, through vicarious observation (e.g., the person witnesses another person being bitten), or through informational transmission (e.g., the person hears from someone else that dogs are dangerous).

The form of associative learning that is most critical to the development of a fear response is known as "classical conditioning," which occurs when a stimulus becomes associated with an involuntary response. This concept is most closely associated with Ivan Pavlov (1849–1936), a Russian physiologist, who discovered classical conditioning accidentally. Pavlov was studying digestion in dogs when he noticed that the dogs in his laboratory began to salivate in response to the technician who brought their food and not merely in the presence of the food itself. Expanding on this research, Pavlov demonstrated that if he repeatedly gave his dogs food while also ringing a bell, the dogs eventually salivated when the bell was presented alone, and no food was given. In the terminology of classical conditioning, Pavlov had taken a sound that had previously been neutral to the dogs, and made it into a conditioned stimulus, meaning that it now elicited a conditioned response (salivation).

Whereas Pavlov's research provided evidence of classical conditioning in animals, John B. Watson (1878–1958) attempted to demonstrate the applicability of these principles in humans. In 1920, Watson and Rayner published the results of an experiment that they conducted on an infant, whom they referred to as Little Albert. Albert, an orphan, was recruited to participate at nine months old from the hospital where he was being raised. Watson wanted to determine whether it was possible to condition Albert to fear a previously neutral stimulus (in this case, a white rat). Believing that children had an innate (i.e., unconditioned) fearful response to loud noises, Watson hypothesized that he could condition Albert to fear the rat by repeatedly presenting the rat at the same time as a fear-inducing loud noise.

Before the conditioning began, Watson presented Albert with various stimuli, such as a white rat, a monkey, and white cotton wool. Albert responded to these objects with curiosity and did not show any signs of fear, meaning that these were neutral stimuli. In the next phase, a loud noise was generated by striking a steel bar with a hammer, which frightened Albert and made him cry. Albert's tearful response to the sound demonstrated that without any training needed, the loud noise acted as an unconditioned stimulus and provoked Albert's unconditioned response of fear.

Now that he had established that Albert responded to loud noises with fear and that he was not afraid of rats before the study, Watson set out to condition the now-11-month-old Albert to fear white rats by presenting the white rat and the loud noise at the same time. Albert initially reached out to touch the rat, but as he did so, the experimenters struck the metal bar, which scared Albert. They paired the noise with the rat three times, waited a week, and then paired the rat and sound four more times. They then presented Albert with the rat and did not make any noise. As one might predict, Albert responded to the rat by crying and crawling away, which meant that Watson had succeeded in conditioning Albert to fear something of which he had not been afraid one week before. Watson also demonstrated that although he had only been conditioned to fear the rat, Albert's fear had spread to other objects that shared some physical characteristics with the rat, such as a white rabbit, a white fur coat, white cotton, and even Watson's gray hair. Watson had intended to try to use further conditioning procedures to eliminate the fears that Albert had learned, but Albert was adopted and left the hospital before Watson had the opportunity.

Obviously, the Little Albert study seems highly unethical when viewed from a modern perspective. Nonetheless, it provides a useful example of how people come to develop extreme fears of certain objects and situations. It also demonstrates that fear can generalize to objects that are perceived as similar to the original stimulus that evoked the fear response. This explains why some people who have been bitten by a German Shepherd can develop a fear of all dogs, and not only to members of the offending breed.

As discussed earlier, classical conditioning describes how a stimulus generates a fear response. To explain how this fear turns into a phobia that is sustained over time, we must introduce another form of associative learning, which is known as operant conditioning. Unlike classical conditioning, which involves the association of a stimulus with an involuntary response that is "hard-wired" into the biology of the organism, operant conditioning refers to learning that involves voluntary actions that are based on the consequences of a behavior.

B. F. Skinner (1904–1990) was a psychologist whose work was especially foundational in developing the principles of operant conditioning. Skinner's research involved placing animals, such as rodents and birds, into a device called an "operant conditioning chamber", otherwise known as a Skinner Box. The animals were taught to perform a particular action, such as pushing a lever, in response to certain stimuli, such as sound or light. The animal might be rewarded with a food pellet for a correct response and punished with an electric shock for an incorrect response.

In this way, Skinner was able to test how animals change their behavior in response to rewards and punishments. He used the term "reinforcer" to describe any consequence that increased the likelihood or strength of a behavioral response and the term "punisher" to describe any consequence that decreased the likelihood or weakened a behavioral response. Skinner divided reinforcers into "positive reinforcers" and "negative reinforcers." Positive reinforcers increased a behavior by providing something pleasant (e.g., a rat rewarded with a food pellet), while negative reinforcers increased a behavior by removing something aversive (e.g., the rat might press a lever which stops a loud noise or an electric shock).

Research suggests that negative reinforcement is particularly important in the development of phobias. As an example, imagine that Mike, who had previously been a confident public speaker, is asked unexpectedly to speak at the end of a meeting he's attending. Up until a few weeks ago, this wouldn't have bothered him, but Mike is still feeling embarrassed because his boss was critical of his last presentation. Mike notices his heart racing, begins to feel sick to his stomach, and decides to quickly exit the meeting. Of course, Mike feels better soon after leaving the room, but his anxiety about appearing unprepared prevents him from returning to the meeting. In this example, Mike's behavior (leaving the room) was negatively reinforced by the reduction of his distress once he had escaped the situation.

Mike, worried about how his boss had responded to his quick exit, might ask his secretary to inform his boss that he had a scheduling conflict and couldn't attend the next meeting. This avoidance behavior would reduce Mike's anxiety, thereby negatively reinforcing the behavior and increasing the likelihood that Mike will cope with future stressors through escape and avoidance. Mike's fear, which started out as a response to a particular stimulus (his boss), begins to generalize to other situations that remind him of the original event that evoked fear. In this way, the principles of classical conditioning explain how Mike's initial fear response is generated, while principles of operant conditioning explain how the fear response is maintained, strengthened, and generalized to the point that it becomes a diagnosable phobia.

✦✜✦

Signs, Symptoms, and Diagnosis

15. When does normal anxiety become a disorder?

Despite the discomfort that they often cause, anxiety and fear are crucial for survival. These emotions provide us with information; they alert us to a danger or threat. As with many human traits, levels of anxiety lie on a continuum, with some people having low levels of anxiety, some having high anxiety, and most falling somewhere in the middle. There is no universally agreed-upon method to decide where normal ends and pathological begins, and the boundaries are often fuzzy. If this is the case, then how does someone determine whether his or her anxiety has become problematic and might require treatment?

The answer is that anxiety becomes a problem when its duration is too long, when its intensity is too high, or when it occurs too frequently. The physiology of problematic anxiety is no different from that of normal anxiety, but what differs is that in problematic anxiety, the emotional response happens in situations in which it is not appropriate or effective. When the duration, intensity, and frequency of anxiety cause impairment or lead to significant distress, an individual may be diagnosed with an anxiety disorder.

In some cases, it is immediately apparent to clinicians, family members, and the individual that he or she is suffering from an anxiety disorder. For example, imagine that Bob experiences daily panic attacks that force him to stay at home for weeks at a time. His paralyzing fear eventually costs him his job, and he will soon be evicted from his home because he can no longer afford the rent. In such a situation, there is little doubt that most reasonable people would recognize that Bob's anxiety falls outside the bounds of "normal," and that he would benefit from professional help. Similarly, if someone is afraid of large dogs, but can tolerate being a few feet away from them without becoming overly distressed, most people would likely agree that this fear is relatively normal and that they probably don't need treatment for anxiety.

Most real-world situations, however, are much less straightforward than the examples described earlier, and in such cases, even specialists often disagree about whether a person's anxiety is severe enough to warrant a diagnosis. Published in 2013, the *Diagnostic and Statistical Manual of Mental Disorders, Fifth Edition* (*DSM-5*) provides clinicians and researchers with sets of criteria, or rules, to help guide them in differentiating normal anxiety from an anxiety disorder. (See Question 16 titled "How are anxiety disorders diagnosed?" for more information on the diagnostic process.)

To determine whether someone's anxiety rises to the level of being a disorder, the problem must be assessed along several dimensions. First, the anxiety must lead the individual to experience high levels of distress and/ or must interfere with his or her ability to fulfill important social or occupational roles. As an example, if Katie becomes terrified at the sight of lions, but she lives in Kansas and can avoid the zoo without any negative consequences, then her anxiety probably would not merit a diagnosis or require treatment.

Second, the anxiety must be out of proportion to the actual threat. To continue the admittedly ridiculous example described earlier, if Katie saw a news report saying that a lion had escaped from a passing circus and was scratching at her back door, then her terror would be understandable given the real threat posed by the situation. Obviously, it would not make sense to diagnose an anxiety disorder under such conditions. If anything, a *lack* of fear would be a cause for concern in this situation.

Third, the anxiety must last long enough to indicate that the problem requires treatment and that it is unlikely to get better spontaneously. Even if the lion had been captured and the circus was far away, most people could probably understand if Katie was unable to leave her house the next day due to residual fear. Would her avoidance of leaving the house still be considered reasonable one week later? How about one year later? Ten years later? Though people might disagree about how long Katie could spend in her house before she would need treatment, it seems likely that most would agree that at a certain point, Katie's behavior would shift from a reasonable response to a scary experience to a sign of a diagnosable problem that requires professional support.

Finally, the anxiety must also be out of proportion given the individual's age. As they progress from infancy through adolescence, children frequently exhibit intense fears that are characteristic of their age group. From ages two to six, children often fear animals and insects, darkness, death, natural events (e.g., thunderstorms), and monsters or imaginary creatures. Between the ages of six and ten, children tend to fear separation from parents, and school-related fears often crop up in this age group. Between the ages of 10 and 13, children begin to understand that death is inevitable and final, and fears involving danger and death become more frequent in this age range. Adolescents aged 14 to 17 tend to fear the loss of social status and worry about how they are evaluated by their peers.

It is important to note that the line between normal and pathological differs depending on cultural and historical context. A deep fear of witchcraft would have been normal in Salem, Massachusetts, around the time of the Salem witch trials. In fact, the absence of such fear might have been a sign of pathology and could have resulted in accusations of witchcraft. Fast forward to Salem, Massachusetts, of the present day, and an intense fear of witches and demonic possession would be viewed a sign of pathology.

Though the *DSM-5* has helped clinicians and patients by providing a standardized method for determining whether an individual has a clinical disorder, one must also bear in mind that these criteria are largely arbitrary. For example, to qualify for a diagnosis of generalized anxiety disorder, the *DSM-5* requires that an individual must experience three out of six relevant symptoms for at least six months. Why three out of six symptoms instead of four out of six? Why six months instead of one month, or three months, or a year? The *DSM-5* is a useful tool, but mental health professionals, policymakers, and the public must remember that the diagnoses are useful constructions in this moment in history and in this society, and do not point to any objective, physical reality.

16. How are anxiety disorders diagnosed?

Psychiatric diagnoses are provided by a medical doctor or qualified mental health professional after a thorough assessment. Psychiatric assessments have several goals, which include identifying the primary (i.e., most important) diagnosis, ruling out diagnoses that don't apply, and identifying comorbid conditions. Accurate diagnoses are crucial for guiding decisions about which treatment options to pursue and for selecting participants to be included or excluded from research studies. Diagnostic evaluations can involve interviews with the patient and family members and may also involve the use of standardized measures, such as self-report or parent-report questionnaires.

Questions advance from the broad to the specific as hypotheses develop about the nature of a patient's problems. Assessments should be thorough and systematic since a patient's initial complaint could direct an interviewer toward one diagnosis, when further questioning would have revealed a significant problem that a client didn't consider relevant or was uncomfortable discussing unless directly asked. People with specific phobias, for example, sometimes struggle to say the name of what they fear, those with post-traumatic stress disorder (PTSD) may be too overwhelmed with emotion to report having experienced a trauma, and those with obsessive-compulsive disorder (OCD) might not volunteer information due to a belief that their thoughts are perverse or shameful. Evaluators must, therefore, be careful to ask questions sensitively, communicating that the patient will not be forced to answer any questions, but also that the professional needs to know that an issue is present to make sure that the appropriate diagnosis is identified.

As is the case for all mental health issues, anxiety disorders are diagnosed through a multistep assessment process:

- Step 1: The clinician asks general "screening" questions to assess anxiety, worry, stress, and fear. If the client reports anxiety symptoms, the clinician will explore the topic in greater detail. Questions could include the following: "When did you first notice increased anxiety?" "Do you find that you're avoiding anything due to fear?" "How would you rate your recent anxiety on a scale of 1–10?"
- Step 2: The clinician asks questions to determine whether the anxiety is likely to be related to a medical condition, substance abuse, or another psychiatric disorder. (See Question 19 titled "Are there other conditions that can be confused with anxiety disorders?" for more information on this topic.) If it appears that the anxiety is, in fact, caused by one of these conditions, then an anxiety disorder is not diagnosed. If, on the other hand, these conditions are ruled out, then an anxiety disorder diagnosis may be considered.
- Step 3: As the interviewer begins narrowing down the list of potential diagnoses, he or she asks increasingly specific questions to determine

which—if any—diagnoses apply to the client. As noted in the previous section, the clinician refers to the *DSM-5* to guide diagnosis. The *DSM-5* offers a list of all psychiatric diagnoses, as well as research-supported information on each diagnosis, including risk factors, prevalence data, and comorbidity data. The *DSM-5* provides a set of diagnostic criteria for each disorder. These criteria are essentially rules that delineate who can and cannot be diagnosed with a specific disorder.

For example, the *DSM-5* provides a set of seven criteria, labeled "A" through "G," which define the diagnosis of specific phobia and which are paraphrased as follows: Criterion A indicates that the individual must experience "marked fear or anxiety" related to a specific situation or object (such as dogs, bridges, and clowns). Criterion B states that the stimulus must "almost always" provoke fear or anxiety. Criterion C tells us that the person must make efforts to avoid the stimulus and/or must only be able to endure the situation with high levels of fear or anxiety. Criterion D states that the fear or anxiety must be disproportionate to the actual threat. Criterion E says that a specific phobia can only be diagnosed if the problem has persisted for at least six months. Criterion F states that the person must experience high levels of distress and/or impairment in functioning because of his or her fear, anxiety, or avoidance of the stimulus. Criterion G informs us that people can only be diagnosed with a specific phobia if the problem cannot be better explained as a symptom of a different disorder (e.g., a fear of germs related to a need for cleanliness might be better explained by an OCD diagnosis rather than a diagnosis of a specific phobia of germs).

Criteria such as these provide the clinician or researcher with a set of "checkboxes" that guide decisions about whether a client or research participant may be diagnosed with a particular disorder. Does Jack report extreme anxiety about dogs, after almost having been killed by a dog last year? If Jack's symptoms also warrant a diagnosis of PTSD, then Criterion G for specific phobia tells us that he can't also receive a diagnosis of specific phobia. Does Ella report high levels of anxiety about flying, which started after a moderately turbulent flight two weeks ago? Criterion E tells us that she can't be diagnosed with a specific phobia because the fear must be present for six months or longer. Does Liam feel extremely anxious around cats but never interact with them because he lives and works in a gated community that doesn't allow pets? If so, Criterion F tells us that the diagnosis would not be applied because Liam isn't experiencing significant distress and it is not interfering with his life. If, however, Liam has chosen to reside in this community to avoid cats, and he is unable to socialize with friends outside the gated community because he would have to pass by a billboard featuring a large picture of a cat, then the diagnosis of specific phobia would likely be appropriate.

In reality, the lines between the various conditions are much less clean than one might assume given the specificity of the diagnostic criteria. Assessment of anxiety disorders is made harder by the fact that the same symptoms can occur in multiple anxiety disorders. For example, the presence of panic attacks could indicate that someone has panic disorder, but panic attacks are common in those with specific phobias, social anxiety disorder, depression, and certain medical problems.

Furthermore, many people who have an anxiety disorder have more than one psychiatric condition. When a patient has a comorbid condition, the clinician must determine which diagnosis is most important and should be treated first. Many factors can influence this decision, including the patient's preferences, the clinician's impression about which diagnosis is generating the most impairment or distress, and which problem is most likely to respond to treatment. The clinician may also determine that unless a particular problem is dealt with first, it will prevent the patient from engaging in treatment (as is often the case with severe depression).

Despite the precise definitions provided by the *DSM-5*, it is evident that assessment rests on the use of objective criteria and the subjective judgment of the evaluator. Whatever its shortcomings, the *DSM-5* attempts to ensure that professionals are referring to the same entity when they discuss a diagnosis, and it represents a tremendous improvement over the anarchy that prevailed in the years before the inclusion of diagnostic criteria in the *DSM-III*.

17. How does anxiety cause people to "choke" under pressure?

It was the third set of the 1993 Wimbledon tennis tournament. Jana Novotna, leading Steffi Graf 4–1, was only a few points from winning the championship. Novotna, ahead 40–30 in the sixth game, appeared to have an insurmountable lead. Novotna double-faulted, making it 40–40. She lost the next point and then lost the subsequent point (and game) on a shot into the net. Now, it was 4–2. She lost the next game easily to Graf, making it 4–3. It was Novotna's turn to serve. She lost the game after double-faulting three times in a row. 4–4. It was Graf's turn to serve, and Novotna didn't score a single point. 4–5. Graf took the next game and won the championship.

Novotna's Wimbledon loss is one of the most famous examples of "choking," a term that refers to a breakdown in performance under high pressure, despite having the skills to succeed under normal circumstances. How can we explain this phenomenon?

The answer to this question involves two interrelated concepts. The first is the Yerkes-Dodson law, which describes the relationship between physiological arousal and performance. This law suggests that to complete a task, an individual requires at least enough arousal to be awake and alert. The more complicated the task, the greater the arousal needed to help the individual concentrate on the task. At the same time, increased arousal is only helpful up to a certain point, beyond which greater arousal makes it difficult to concentrate and leads the individual to make more errors.

As an illustration of this point, research has shown that when people are completing simple, repetitive tasks, they tend to perform better when someone is observing them because being observed increases their level of physiological arousal. Increased alertness translates to greater attention, which in turn leads to improved performance. The presence of an observer has the opposite impact when the individual is performing a task that is more complicated or that he or she has not practiced to the point of proficiency. In this case, the arousal from being observed, in combination with the mental effort required to complete a complex task, "overshoots" the optimal level of arousal, and leads to difficulties with concentration and performance.

The second, related idea that explains the phenomenon of choking comes from the work of Daniel Kahneman, who won the Nobel Prize in economics in 2002. Kahneman suggested that people make decisions using two distinct modes of thinking. "System 1" responds automatically and intuitively, without conscious control or awareness. "System 2" is active when we become consciously aware of our thoughts and when we act with intention. Whereas System 1 enables quick reactions, System 2 is slower and more deliberative.

To illustrate the difference between these systems, if you have been driving for a few months, you can probably start your car without having to consciously review all the steps involved. You just get in the car and do it. This is an example of System 1—the process is so well learned that it no longer requires conscious processing. If, however, you were asked to sequentially list each of the steps involved in starting your car, this would involve the deliberate consideration used by System 2 (e.g., "Do I put on my seatbelt after I put the key into the ignition but before I turn the key?").

To explain how the interplay of these systems leads to choking, imagine a child learning to play the piano. During the first lessons, a teacher might show the child how to sit, where to place her fingers, how to count the beats in a measure, and so on. Through repetition, the child eventually learns these behaviors to the point that he or she becomes automatic and intuitive. As time goes on and expertise develops, the child may lose the ability to access the information verbally; his or her behavior becomes so automatic that he or she cannot explain it verbally to a layperson. This compartmentalization of skills partially explains why an incredible athlete, musician, or mathematician may not make a great teacher.

When people are under pressure, they become more self-conscious and anxious about the possible consequences of failure. They begin to shift from System 1, which implicitly knows how to play piano, to System 2, which is poorly equipped for rapidly guiding a complex sequence of behaviors. System 2 leads people to monitor their actions more carefully and to think consciously about the steps needed to perform a task. This is problematic because in many domains, including sports and music, successful performance relies on automatic, learned behaviors. Through years of repetition, these skills have been transferred to System 1 and are no longer accessible to the conscious mind. Simply put, anxiety provokes the individual to use the "wrong" cognitive system, causing errors that would not have been made if he or she used the automatic system that usually guides a well-learned behavior.

18. How is anxiety related to depression?

In a parody article published by the Canadian Medical Association in 2000, the authors asserted that each character featured in the "Winnie the Pooh" children's series suffered from a diagnosable mental illness. Tigger's risky and socially intrusive behaviors, the authors said, indicated that he had attention-deficit hyperactivity disorder (ADHD), predominately hyperactive/impulsive subtype. Winnie was also diagnosed with ADHD, albeit of the inattentive subtype. Rabbit had narcissistic personality disorder, and Owl had dyslexia. The authors expressed concern that Christopher Robin was in the early stages of developing gender identity disorder (though subsequent experts and Internet commenters have diagnosed him with schizophrenia or dissociative identity disorder).

Of interest to this question are Piglet and Eeyore. Piglet's excessive worry, restlessness, problems with concentration, physiological arousal to anxiety-provoking situations, and sleep difficulties are consistent with a diagnosis of generalized anxiety disorder (GAD). Eeyore's low energy, apathy, and hopelessness are suggestive of depression. The most prominent symptoms of major depressive disorder (MDD) are persistent feelings of sadness and "anhedonia," which is defined as the loss of interest/pleasure in previously enjoyed activities. Other symptoms of MDD include changes in appetite and/or weight, changes in sleeping patterns, changes in activity levels, fatigue, feelings of worthlessness or excessive guilt, problems with attention and/or decision-making, and recurrent thoughts about death and/or suicidal thinking or behavior.

Eeyore and Piglet appear to represent the archetypal versions of their respective disorders, with Eeyore being as intolerably depressed as Piglet is painfully anxious. Their characters are distinct from one another, and their behavior and thought patterns are consistent over time. Unlike the tidy packages of anxiety and depression seen in these fictional characters, researchers have found that anxiety and depression are strongly associated with one another. People who have depression are also likely to have an anxiety disorder, and those with an anxiety disorder are also likely to have depression (i.e., the conditions are highly comorbid). Among the anxiety disorders, GAD is most likely to be comorbid with depression, and agoraphobia and specific phobias are least likely. One study found that out of 670 patients who had experienced depression at some point in their lives, 95 percent had also experienced an anxiety disorder.

There are many potential answers to the question of why there is such a strong relationship between anxiety and depression. One theory is that anxiety may directly cause depression. In this theory, depression is the long-term negative consequence that one suffers for repeatedly avoiding anxiety-provoking situations. As their anxiety worsens, people may avoid activities that they previously enjoyed. For example, a high school student with social anxiety disorder might stop eating with her friends because, after spilling her soda all over the floor during lunch the previous week, she fears walking through the crowded school cafeteria. As her avoidance intensifies, she has fewer opportunities to experience positive emotions and is therefore unable to disconfirm her negative self-judgments (e.g., because she eats alone, she does not see the evidence that her friends enjoy her company, and begins to imagine that people dislike her). Indeed, the relationship between anxiety and depression is strongest when the individual has social anxiety disorder or panic disorder, both of which lead people to refrain from activities that might bring them comfort.

Another possible explanation for the relationship between anxiety and depression is that they are different manifestations of the same underlying illness. Some argue that whether someone is diagnosed with anxiety versus depression depends upon when in life the person is assessed. Anxiety disorders tend to have an earlier age of onset than depression, and researchers have found that among those who develop depression, most had already experienced an anxiety disorder. The presence of an anxiety disorder has been identified as the most significant predictor of later depression, raising the likelihood of depression by 2 to 14 times the normal rate. Consequently, when assessed earlier in life, someone might have more symptoms of anxiety than depression, and when that same person is evaluated later in life, symptoms of depression might be more prominent.

There is, however, strong evidence against the idea that anxiety disorders and depression reflect a single illness, leading most experts to conclude that the differences between them are sufficient to justify separating them into different diagnostic categories. For example, one study looked at physiological changes in response to a laboratory test designed to induce stress. Participants were divided into three groups: those with "pure" anxiety (specifically panic disorder and social anxiety disorder), "pure" depression, or comorbid anxiety and depression. The researchers found that each of the three groups responded to stress differently, indicating that there are meaningful distinctions between those with anxiety, depression, and comorbid anxiety and depression.

While most anxiety disorders can be distinguished from depression, GAD is so highly correlated with depression that genetic studies suggest that they may be one illness. This makes sense, given the extent to which their symptoms overlap. Sleep disturbance, restlessness, fatigue, and concentration difficulties are listed among the diagnostic criteria for both disorders in the *DSM-5*, which may artificially increase comorbidity because the same symptoms are counted twice. Indeed, a 2012 study found that people with comorbid GAD and MDD reported that they experienced the four overlapping symptoms more often than the nonoverlapping symptoms, suggesting that the high comorbidity between GAD and MDD may be partially due to poorly constructed diagnostic criteria, which weaken the boundaries between the conditions.

To explain how anxiety disorders and depression are similar to one another and also how they differ, researchers Lee Anna Clark and David Watson proposed their tripartite model of anxiety and depression. Clark and Watson recategorized the symptoms of anxiety and depression into three factors:

- Negative affect: a dimension of emotional experience characterized by distress and dissatisfaction, which includes emotional states such as anger, guilt, sadness, fear, and disgust.
- Positive affect: the opposite of negative affect, it is comprised of pleasant emotional states including happiness, joy, and confidence.
- Physiological hyperarousal: the activation of the fight-or-flight response, which includes shortness of breath, dizziness, and rapid heart rate.

The presence or absence of these factors determines whether an individual has an anxiety disorder, depression, or both. High levels of negative affect, which can include sadness and anxiety, are seen in both anxiety disorders and depression. This tendency toward high negative affect is hypothesized to be the common ingredient between these conditions, and it explains the comorbidity between them. Low levels of positive affect are characteristic of depression, but not anxiety disorders. Anhedonia, which refers to a lack of interest or pleasure in activities that one used to enjoy, is a symptom of depression. Anhedonia is not typical of those with anxiety disorders, who are usually able to enjoy activities provided that they don't trigger significant anxiety. Physiological hyperarousal is more characteristic of anxiety disorders than depression.

Though people with anxiety disorders and those with depression are both prone to experience negative emotion, they tend to respond to these emotions with different patterns of thinking. Whereas those with anxiety disorders tend to have thoughts that involve worry about anticipated danger, those with depression are more likely to report thoughts related to hopelessness, low self-worth, and loss. People who have comorbid anxiety and depression report having both types of thoughts.

The consequences of comorbid anxiety and depression are significant. People with comorbid anxiety and depression have more severe symptoms than those with only one of these conditions, their illnesses are more chronic, and they have more difficulties with work and in intimate relationships. They are slower to respond to psychotherapy and psychiatric medications and are more sensitive to side effects from drugs. They have poorer physical functioning and experience more pain than patients with many other chronic medical problems. Such patients are also at greater risk for suicide attempts. Indeed, one study found that those with comorbid depression and panic disorder were four times more likely to have made a suicide attempt than those with panic disorder alone.

Research in this area is ongoing, but thankfully, the first-line treatments for anxiety, depression, and comorbid anxiety and depression are fairly similar, meaning that the most distressing symptoms are likely to be targeted regardless of the specific diagnosis that a person receives. Treatments are likely to involve antidepressant medications, which can be helpful in reducing symptoms of anxiety and depression, and/or cognitive-behavioral therapy, which is flexible based on the needs of the client and can, therefore, be adapted to address comorbid conditions. Accurate diagnosis is helpful, however, since it allows the clinician to set reasonable expectations for the pace of progress and also alerts the clinician to the need to follow up with the patient after treatment has concluded to monitor for recurrence of symptoms.

19. Are there other conditions that can be confused with anxiety disorders?

People who seek help for anxiety require a careful assessment, as their symptoms can sometimes be caused by factors other than an anxiety disorder. These may include a physical condition whose symptoms mimic those of an anxiety disorder, the presence of another physical or psychiatric condition that impacts the anxiety symptoms, side effects or withdrawal from a prescribed medication, or substance abuse.

A thorough evaluation will lead to one of four possible outcomes:

1. The client's anxiety is the primary and only pertinent problem.
2. The anxiety is caused purely by a physical condition, medication, or substance.
3. The anxiety has been aggravated by a comorbid psychiatric condition, physical illness, medication, or substance.
4. The individual has anxiety and other conditions, but the anxiety is unrelated to these other issues.

As indicated in the second and third of the possibilities listed earlier, people sometimes seek treatment for anxiety, only to find that their symptoms were being caused or exacerbated by a physiological problem. For example, symptoms of heart arrhythmia, asthma, hyperthyroidism, epilepsy, vertigo, head injury, pregnancy, anemia, and some vitamin deficiencies may be misdiagnosed as symptoms of anxiety. For this reason, experts recommend that patients who are struggling with anxiety should get a comprehensive medical examination to rule out physical causes.

Clinicians are more likely to suspect a physiological cause when someone reports a sudden onset of anxiety without any prior history of similar problems, recent life stressors, or family history of anxiety. Anxiety is also more likely to have a biological cause if it started or worsened at the same time as some other physical symptom. Headaches, strange perceptual experiences (e.g., numbness, tingling, hallucinations, dissociation), or significant changes in cognitive functioning could indicate a neurological problem if their onset overlaps with the emergence of anxiety. If, for example, a patient with no prior history of anxiety began to experience severe symptoms soon after a concussion, it is reasonable to consider the possibility that his or her emotional distress is related to the lingering effects of head trauma.

Experts warn that some medications and substances can cause symptoms that are hard to distinguish from those of anxiety disorders. Agitation, nausea, and dizziness are common experiences in anxiety, but they are also side effects of codeine, a medication widely prescribed for pain relief. Similarly, caffeine can cause rapid heart rate, heart palpitations, shakiness, and dizziness—symptoms that are also commonly experienced in anxiety disorders. Other medications that are known to occasionally provoke anxiety symptoms include insulin, statins, thyroid medications, steroids, oral contraceptives, and antihistamines. Stimulants, including caffeine and nicotine, can cause anxiety during the period of intoxication when people ingest too high a dosage. Even at low doses, stimulants can cause anxiety if people use them when they are already under stress. Alcohol and marijuana can alleviate stress in the short term, but their heavy or prolonged use frequently leads to symptoms of anxiety.

20. Is homophobia an anxiety disorder?

In 1972, psychologist George Weinberg (1929–2017) coined the term "homophobia," which he defined as "the dread of being in close quarters with homosexuals." The introduction of this term is considered a watershed moment in the history of the gay rights movement. Up until its removal in 1974, "homosexuality" was listed as a mental illness in the *DSM-II*. The inclusion of homosexuality as an officially sanctioned psychiatric diagnosis lent scientific legitimacy to the idea that gay people needed to be "cured" of their sexual preferences. The concept of homophobia turned this idea on its head by suggesting that the pathology did not lie in gay people, but rather in those who harbored prejudice against gay people.

The value of homophobia as a conceptual tool for furthering tolerance is not under dispute. But is the term accurate? Does homophobia qualify as an anxiety disorder?

Consider the following examples: A person who has arachnophobia (fear of spiders) sees a spider on the floor and immediately backs away in fear. Someone with trypanophobia (fear of needles) avoids going to the doctor for years due to fear of getting an injection. Those with nyctophobia (fear of the dark) sleep with the lights on. People with coulrophobia (fear of clowns) refuse to attend children's birthday parties. The key similarity among these conditions, which are all forms of specific phobia, is that sufferers experience extreme fear when confronted with the object of their phobia, and that they attempt to avoid the stimulus or endure it with intense distress.

In terms of emotional content and behavioral manifestations, homophobia is very different from the specific phobias described earlier. Instead of intense fear, homophobia is characterized mainly by anger or disgust; instead of avoidance, homophobia has been associated with shocking acts of cruelty and violence. Homophobia has been implicated as a cause or contributing factor for a shooting attack at a gay nightclub in Orlando that resulted in 49 deaths, the torture and murder of gay people in Chechnya, and statutes that criminalize and punish homosexual behavior in countries around the world. The violence associated with homophobia suggests that it is not an anxiety disorder. Instead, because it is expressed primarily through actions arising from anger, disgust, and hostility, homophobia is more accurately conceptualized as a variant of prejudice.

21. Is it possible to die from a panic attack?

Given the fact that many of the physical symptoms of panic attack seem superficially similar to those of a heart attack, it makes sense for those in the midst of a panic attack to fear that they are truly at risk of dying. Consequently, people with panic disorder tend to use more medical resources, including laboratory tests, visits to the doctor, and medical procedures, than those without panic attacks. Panic attacks can be a symptom of other conditions, such as hyperthyroidism, and can result from the use or abuse of stimulants, including caffeine, attention-deficit hyperactivity disorder (ADHD) medications, cocaine, and methamphetamines. The likelihood of panic disorder is higher in people suffering from certain cardiovascular and respiratory conditions, but it is uncommon for these conditions to directly cause panic attacks. Because of these complicated interactions with medical problems, experts recommend that people experiencing panic attacks should be evaluated by a physician to rule out any medical causes.

With the earlier caveat in mind, as a general rule, otherwise healthy people really cannot die from a panic attack. Recent studies do suggest a link between panic attacks and heart disease, but this relationship has been demonstrated only in older adults. This research does not prove causality and therefore can't tell us whether panic attacks lead to heart disease, heart disease leads to panic attacks, or some other factor leads to both.

Treatment

22. How are anxiety disorders treated?

Treatments for anxiety disorders fall into a few broad categories, including psychotherapy, stress management techniques, pharmacotherapy (i.e., treatment using medication), and complementary and alternative medicine. Treatments can vary greatly in their effectiveness, and there is often a significant lag between the time that research on a given treatment is published and the time that clinicians start applying the results in their work with patients. Because of this gap, clinicians sometimes treat patients using outdated medications or therapeutic techniques, as they are unaware that a more effective treatment is available.

Experts have developed guidelines to help clinicians offer recommendations based on the best evidence available. These guidelines are meant to counteract the tendency to rely on intuition, anecdotal evidence, or outdated theories to guide decisions. There are slight differences between the various guidelines, but they consistently suggest that effective treatment is likely to consist of medications, psychotherapy, or some combination of the two. While there are some exceptions (e.g., specific phobia, for which pharmacotherapy is not recommended), research mostly supports the idea that psychotherapy and medication are equally effective as stand-alone treatments. Some studies suggest that a combination of therapy and psychiatric drugs is more effective than either treatment separately, whereas others have found that combined treatment is no better than either treatment alone.

Clinical guidelines advocate the use of cognitive-behavioral therapy (CBT) over other forms of psychotherapy because CBT has more experimental support. For patients who choose medication, guidelines for most anxiety disorders recommend selective serotonin reuptake inhibitor (SSRI) medications, but benzodiazepines are sometimes indicated for conditions such as panic disorder. When people do not respond to SSRIs, guidelines usually recommend that patients be tapered off the first medication and then try another SSRI rather than being prescribed multiple medications at the same time.

An influential set of guidelines developed in the United Kingdom suggests that after a patient has been diagnosed, the clinician should evaluate symptom severity to determine next steps. If the problem is mild, the clinician recommends a period of "watchful waiting," during which the patient and professional see if symptoms improve on their own, or the clinician might recommend CBT delivered via computer. If the anxiety is judged to be moderate, the guidelines recommend CBT, pharmacotherapy, or both; the recommendation for severe anxiety is combined CBT and pharmacotherapy. The decision about whether to choose CBT, medication, or a combined treatment may be guided by the patient's preferences, the availability of trained therapists in the area, and the patient's ability to attend therapy regularly.

23. What is psychotherapy?

Psychotherapy, which is also called "therapy" or "talk therapy," is a broad term that describes the treatment of mental disorders using psychological means. In the United States, psychotherapy can be provided by licensed professionals (e.g., clinical psychologists, registered psychiatric nurses, clinical social workers, and psychiatrists), but it can also be provided without a license (e.g., religious clergy, drug and alcohol counselors). It is, therefore, a good idea for anyone seeking psychotherapy to ask the professional about whether and by whom they are licensed, as a poorly trained therapist can do more harm than good. Psychotherapy is contrasted with pharmacotherapy, which refers to treatments using medication, and is (with few exceptions) provided only by physicians and nurses. Psychiatrists are medical doctors who, after attending medical school, have received specialized training in the treatment of mental illness.

There are many approaches to psychotherapy, and treatment can differ widely depending on a therapist's training, style, and personality. During their training, therapists are exposed to theories that seek to explain how mental health problems develop and how they are best resolved. The understanding that a therapist adopts, also known as his or her theoretical orientation, guides the therapist's approach to treatment. A therapist's theoretical orientation impacts many aspects of treatment, including his or her attitude toward offering direct advice, the therapist's willingness to disclose information about his or her own life, and the extent to which the therapist guides the session to particular topics versus allowing the client to determine the course of the conversation.

Two of the most well-established forms of therapy are psychodynamic psychotherapy and cognitive-behavioral therapy (CBT). While the terms "CBT" and "psychodynamic psychotherapy" describe a diverse set of techniques and theoretical conceptualizations, there are many differences between the two. Psychodynamic psychotherapy, as an outgrowth of psychoanalysis, is based on the work of Sigmund Freud and his successors. In contrast to CBT, which attempts to reduce problematic symptoms by modifying the thoughts and behaviors that are maintaining the client's anxiety, psychodynamic therapy tends to focus on helping clients develop insight into the unconscious factors that are presumed to be the source of their distress. Symptom reduction in psychodynamic therapy is thought to result from this increased awareness. Some treatments, such as CBT for specific phobias, may be administered in a single session, while others, such as psychoanalysis, can involve three to five meetings per week for many years.

Psychotherapy can be delivered in several different ways. The most common of these, which people typically think of when they hear someone talk about being "in therapy," is individual therapy, in which the patient meets with his or her therapist one-on-one. In most forms of individual therapy, the therapist and patient meet once per week for about an hour, though the frequency and length of sessions can vary depending on the style of therapy and the patient's specific circumstances. When family interactions are relevant, treatment often benefits from the participation of some or all family members. The goals of family participation can range from simply providing family members with guidance as to how they can support the anxious patient more effectively to helping family members develop healthier relationships with one another.

Therapy can also be provided in a group setting, in which multiple clients meet with a therapist at the same time. Group therapy can be extremely beneficial since it reduces the shame that often accompanies mental illness, allows clients to gain support from one another, and can make treatment more affordable. Furthermore, in the case of social anxiety disorder, this format offers the added benefit of giving clients the opportunity to expose themselves to their fears and practice social skills through their participation in the group.

Please note that although there is some controversy regarding which of several approaches is most effective for the treatment of anxiety, we will focus our discussion on CBT, as it is generally considered to be a first-line psychotherapeutic treatment for anxiety disorders.

24. What is cognitive-behavioral therapy, and how is it applied to anxiety?

Cognitive-behavioral therapy (CBT) is the most widely used—and most evidence-supported—treatment for anxiety disorders. The effectiveness of CBT for anxiety disorders has been demonstrated in hundreds of clinical studies, and CBT is recommended in anxiety treatment guidelines published by the National Institute of Mental Health (NIMH) in the United States and by the National Institute for Health and Clinical Excellence (NICE) in the United Kingdom. CBT is a brief (i.e., between 6 and 20 sessions), problem-focused treatment that seeks to alleviate the client's symptoms by modifying the thoughts and behaviors that maintain his or her emotional distress.

CBT represents a combination of concepts drawn from behaviorism and cognitive psychology. The behavioral component of CBT is based on the work of Ivan Pavlov, John Watson, and B. F. Skinner, whose research on learning and conditioning was adapted for use in the treatment of psychiatric disorders by Joseph Wolpe. After behaviorists demonstrated that phobias could be learned through repeated pairings of a previously neutral stimulus with an aversive stimulus (e.g., the Little Albert study, described in Question 14, "How do people develop irrational fears of spiders, dogs, heights, and so on?"), Wolpe next demonstrated that these fears could be extinguished if the previously neutral stimulus was repeatedly presented without the aversive stimulus.

The cognitive component of CBT was developed by Aaron T. Beck and Albert Ellis, who independently recognized the pivotal role of maladaptive thoughts in anxiety and depression. The philosophical roots of cognitive therapy can be traced to the Stoic philosopher Epictetus (55–135 CE), who said, "Men are disturbed not by things, but by the views which they take of things." Cognitive and behavioral therapies were considered different treatments until the 1980s when David M. Clark and David H. Barlow developed treatments for panic disorder that demonstrated the value of merging these two therapies into a single approach, which we now know as CBT.

Since the 1980s, many treatments that fall under the umbrella of CBT have been developed. Despite their differences, all forms of CBT are built around the same key organizing principle, namely, that our experience is shaped by the interaction of our thoughts, emotions, and behaviors. Sometimes referred to as the "CBT model" or the "three-component model," CBT assumes that because the domains of thought, emotion, and behavior are continually influencing one another, a change in one part will necessarily have an impact on the other parts. When, for example, someone inaccurately evaluates a situation as dangerous (the thought) and therefore avoids it (the behavior), his or her fear is likely to increase (the emotion). If the avoidance becomes habitual and the fear becomes intensely distressing, this can culminate in an anxiety disorder. CBT attempts to harness the interconnectivity of thoughts, emotions, and behaviors to bring about positive change. In CBT, the client learns to rationally evaluate the risk posed by the feared situation, which leads to reduced fear and allows them to approach the situation.

To illustrate the CBT model and how it might guide treatment for anxiety, imagine Sam, a 17-year-old student who has had difficulties with social anxiety since moving to a new high school. Sam enters the lunchroom and notices several people laughing as he walks past their table. He thinks "they're laughing at me" (the thought), which leads to heightened anxiety (the emotion). Fearing further embarrassment, Sam leaves the lunchroom (the behavior). In this model, Sam's escape from the lunchroom serves to reduce his distress in the short term, but in the long term, it increases his anxiety by reinforcing his belief that avoidance is his best option for coping with stress. Avoidance robs Sam of the opportunity to make friends, which guarantees continued social isolation.

Though CBT should be applied flexibly to meet the needs of each individual patient, anxiety treatments drawn from this approach will usually share certain features, which include the following:

- **Assessment:** CBT begins with a careful diagnostic assessment. The therapist and client review the list of current problems and decide which issues they should target first. There is no fixed rule for selecting the first treatment target, so therapy could, for example, start with the most distressing problem, the most impairing problem, or the problem that the client finds least intimidating to approach.
- **Psychoeducation:** The therapist teaches the client about the connection between thoughts, emotions, and behaviors; about the nature of

anxiety (i.e., anxiety evolved to protect people from danger, but in modern life, most of the things that make us anxious are not actually dangerous); and provides information about the patient's condition(s).

- **Homework:** CBT typically involves the assignment of homework tasks to be completed in between sessions. These assignments help clients master the skills they are learning through repeated practice in real-world settings, which leads to more rapid and sustained improvement than could be accomplished without homework. Homework can take many forms and could involve tracking fluctuations in the frequency and severity of anxiety, identifying and disputing maladaptive beliefs, and completing daily exposure tasks.

- **Cognitive restructuring:** The client learns to identify, challenge, and finally replace maladaptive thoughts with thoughts that are more rational or helpful.

- **Exposure:** The therapist and client develop an exposure hierarchy, which is a list of feared stimuli from least to most distressing. Someone with a specific phobia of dogs, for instance, could have a hierarchy that ascends from petting a Chihuahua to a pit bull. The client may complete the exposures during therapy sessions, as homework, or both. The client can expose himself or herself to a feared situation using his or her imagination (known as imaginal exposure) or in real life (known as in *vivo* exposure). People may also do interoceptive exposure, which involves exposure to feared physical sensations (e.g., someone with panic disorder can expose himself or herself to dizziness by spinning in a chair).

- **Elimination of safety behaviors:** Though there is some disagreement on the necessity of this component (particularly early in treatment), CBT generally asks clients to stop engaging in safety behaviors. These are subtle avoidance behaviors that are meant to reduce emotional discomfort or to minimize the risk of some feared outcome. For example, people with social anxiety are often uncomfortable attending parties without a close friend they can use as a "home base" in case they feel awkward or overwhelmed. CBT would encourage such a person to get to the party ten minutes before his or her friend arrives so that he or she can learn to manage his or her discomfort without relying on others. (For more on the consequences of avoidance, see Question 27 titled "Is it best for people to avoid the things that make them anxious?")

- **Skills training:** CBT may include relaxation exercises and breathing retraining to teach the client how to lower his or her physiological arousal, social skills training to reduce social anxiety, and problem-solving training to help the client deal more effectively with stressful situations.

Returning to the example of Sam described earlier, a cognitive-behavioral therapist would have many options for how to help Sam reduce his anxiety. In the psychoeducation phase, the therapist would describe the CBT model as it relates to social anxiety, with particular attention to the role of maladaptive cognitions. The therapist would explain that people with social anxiety tend to have a specific set of inaccurate and maladaptive thoughts. Sam would learn that people with social anxiety tend to over-predict the likelihood and seriousness of social rejection. Due to their excessively high standards for success in social situations, as well as their mistaken beliefs that others are watching them closely, people with social anxiety frequently engage in avoidance behaviors that only worsen their distress over time.

Therapy sessions would focus on increasing Sam's awareness of his own "automatic thoughts," which are thoughts or images that seem to pop up quickly and automatically in response to an event. Sam would recognize that in anxiety-provoking social situations, these automatic thoughts were overwhelmingly negative and rarely accurate. This realization would help Sam take a more skeptical approach to his thoughts, and he would begin to see his thoughts as guesses about the world and not as true reflections of reality.

The therapist might also teach Sam about the concept of "cognitive distortions," which are irrational or exaggerated thought patterns that lead people to make inaccurate (and usually negative) interpretations of their experience. By becoming more aware of his cognitive distortions, Sam would recognize that his interpretation that he was being laughed at when he entered the lunchroom was an example of "mind reading," in which he assumed that the other students were laughing directly at him even though he had no evidence that this was the case. Sam might also notice another cognitive distortion called "discounting the positive," in which he labeled himself as an outcast based on only a few negative experiences, but that he had wholly ignored his much more numerous social successes. After learning to identify the errors in thinking that fueled his anxiety, Sam would next learn to dispute these thoughts with evidence.

The therapist might decide to emphasize behavioral strategies at the beginning of treatment or might shift to a behavioral approach after some of the cognitive work had been completed. Sam and his therapist would construct a hierarchy of feared events. Walking through the halls without looking at his phone could be a low-intensity task, raising his hand in a class that he shares with one of the most popular kids in his grade could be a medium-intensity task, and the highest-intensity exposure might involve asking to sit with a group of classmates at lunch. Sam would complete these exposure tasks in order and would review his experience during therapy sessions. With each success, Sam would become less frightened of the next exposure, and before long, his anxiety would likely improve to the point that the final exposures would be much less stressful than Sam could have anticipated before he started therapy.

Through the successful application of cognitive and behavioral strategies, patients are likely to experience a significant reduction in their distress as well as improvements in functioning. CBT concludes when the client has met his or her initial goals for treatment, and when the client is functioning at a level that is sufficient to meet the demands of his or her environment. CBT typically ends by reviewing what the client has learned, planning for how he or she will cope with challenges in the future (which is meant to reduce the risk of relapse), and identifying specific markers that would indicate that the client should return to treatment either for a booster session or for weekly therapy.

25. What kinds of medications are used? How do they work?

There has been a great deal of research on the use of medications to treat anxiety disorders. These drugs fall into several different classes, each of which has a different "mechanism of action," or process by which the medication produces its effect. The categories of anxiety medications include selective serotonin reuptake inhibitors (SSRIs), serotonin-norepinephrine reuptake inhibitors (SNRIs), tricyclic antidepressants (TCAs), monoamine oxidase inhibitors (MAOIs), noradrenergic and specific serotonergic antidepressants (NaSSAs), reversible inhibitors of monoamine oxidase (RIMAs), beta-blockers, and benzodiazepines. While some medications, such as SSRIs, are often prescribed to treat a wide variety of anxiety disorders, others are typically prescribed for specific diagnoses, such as beta-blockers for performance anxiety.

In choosing a specific medication for a particular individual, the prescriber must weigh the potential benefits of a drug against its risks for the person being treated. Beyond evaluating the research base for applying a medication to the client's presenting problem, the prescriber must also consider many other factors. These can include the client's age, history of medical conditions, history of compliance with previous medications, suicide risk, history of substance abuse, and whether the client or a close relative has benefited from a drug in the past.

For example, while benzodiazepines may be helpful as a short-term treatment for panic attacks, they are also highly addictive, and doctors are (or should be) reluctant to prescribe such medications for those who have a recent history of substance abuse. Benzodiazepines may also cause cognitive impairment in older adults. Psychiatrists may be less likely to prescribe SSRIs for individuals who are at risk for bipolar disorder since this class of medications can sometimes trigger manic episodes. As another example, some TCAs have been found to be effective in treating obsessive-compulsive disorder (OCD), but overdoses in this class are more often fatal than SSRIs, and so they must be prescribed very carefully for those who have a history of suicidal thinking or behavior.

Though most medications that are prescribed for the treatment of anxiety have been vetted and approved by the Food and Drug Administration (FDA) specifically to treat mood disorders, others are prescribed "off-label." This term applies when a physician prescribes a medication to treat a condition for which the drug does not have FDA approval, but which the doctor feels will be beneficial based on research or anecdotal evidence. For example, the drug prazosin was approved by the FDA as a treatment for high blood pressure, but it has also been found to be effective in reducing nightmares in those who have post-traumatic stress disorder, a use for which it has not been approved by the FDA.

While a detailed discussion of all the medications and their application to each anxiety disorder is outside the scope of this work, we will review three of the classes that are most widely prescribed for anxiety disorders, which are benzodiazepines, SSRIs, and beta-blockers.

HOW DO ANTIANXIETY MEDICATIONS WORK?

Most antianxiety drugs work by inducing changes that either increase or decrease the availability or action of specific neurotransmitters. Before explaining how these medications exert their influence, it will be useful to quickly review some basic information about the brain.

Put (very) simply, neurotransmitters are chemical messengers that are released into the gap (or synapse) between one neuron and another cell to which it is sending a signal. The neuron sending the signal is referred to as the "presynaptic neuron," while the one receiving the signal is called the "postsynaptic neuron." Scientists do not know how many neurotransmitters exist in total but have identified over 100 thus far. A neurotransmitter acts as either excitatory (increasing the likelihood that the postsynaptic neuron will fire) or inhibitory (decreasing the probability of firing). The firing of the presynaptic neuron, in turn, could lead the postsynaptic neuron to release neurotransmitters into the synapse that it shares with other neurons, resulting in the excitation or inhibition of additional neurons.

After the neurotransmitter has completed its task of communicating with the receiving neuron, the leftover neurotransmitter must be removed from the synapse so that it does not continually bounce into receptors on the postsynaptic cell. The neurotransmitter can be deactivated in a few ways: it can drift away, be removed by glial cell, or be broken down by enzymes released into the synapse. Alternatively, through a process known as reuptake, the neurotransmitter can be reabsorbed and reused by the cell from which it was initially released.

Medications can lead to changes in behavior by altering neurotransmission through several mechanisms. Some drugs, for example, stimulate or block the release of neurotransmitters, while other drugs cause one or more neurotransmitters to be produced in greater or smaller amounts. Medications known as receptor *antagonists* prevent neurotransmitters from binding to their receptors on the postsynaptic neuron by sitting in the space where the neurotransmitters usually bind to their receptors, thereby blocking them from reaching their targets. Medications known as receptor *agonists* bind to a receptor and "trick" the receptor into "thinking" that it is binding with the normal neurotransmitter, which leads the neuron to respond as though the actual neurotransmitter had been released. Other medications increase the effect of a neurotransmitter by impeding its removal from the synapse, which means that the signal from the neurotransmitter has more opportunity to repeatedly "ping" its receptors on the receiving end.

BENZODIAZEPINES

Commonly prescribed benzodiazepines include alprazolam (Xanax), lorazepam (Ativan), clonazepam (Klonopin), and diazepam (Valium). Benzodiazepines work by enhancing the action of a neurotransmitter called gamma-aminobutyric acid (GABA). GABA is an inhibitory neurotransmitter, meaning that it sends a message to other neurons to stop firing. By increasing the efficiency of GABA, benzodiazepines cause the brain to slow down its communication, which in most people induces feelings of calmness and sedation.

Whereas it can take several weeks for an individual to experience reduced anxiety on an SSRI, people are likely to feel the effects of benzodiazepines within a matter of minutes. Because of the speed with which benzodiazepines take effect, they are often prescribed for short-term anxiety management, and may, for example, be used to reduce the intensity and duration of panic attacks. The long-term use of benzodiazepines is a controversial topic; recent research indicates that benzodiazepines become less effective over time, that long-term use leads to tolerance (and potentially fatal withdrawal symptoms if abruptly discontinued), and that long-term use may also result in cognitive problems, sleep difficulties, mood changes, and sexual dysfunction.

Selective Serotonin Reuptake Inhibitors

The SSRIs include such medications as escitalopram (Lexapro), paroxetine (Paxil), fluoxetine (Prozac), and fluvoxamine (Luvox). These drugs work by interfering with the reuptake of serotonin, a neurotransmitter that has been linked to mood. SSRIs block the presynaptic neuron from reabsorbing serotonin after it has been released into the synapse. This increases the amount of time that serotonin molecules are available to bind with the postsynaptic neuron, thereby strengthening the signal being sent by the presynaptic cell.

Interestingly, despite their widespread usage, the exact mechanism by which SSRIs lead to improvements in anxiety and depression is unknown. While it was once believed that anxiety and depression resulted from inadequate levels of serotonin and other neurotransmitters in the brain (the so-called chemical imbalance theory), researchers now see this as incorrect. For example, a 2015 study found that those with social anxiety had *higher* levels of serotonin than healthy controls, suggesting that deficient serotonin production cannot be the cause of this condition. Furthermore, while SSRIs take only minutes to start blocking the reuptake of serotonin, they take several weeks to have a positive impact on mood, which indicates that their effect cannot be explained purely by increased serotonin availability. The complex relationship between SSRI medications, serotonin levels, and mood is further illustrated by research that shows that people often experience an increase in anxiety for the first few weeks of SSRI treatment, and that particularly for the first eight weeks of treatment, SSRI use is associated with an increased suicide risk in children and adolescents.

BETA-BLOCKERS

Beta-blockers, particularly propranolol (Inderal) and atenolol (Tenormin), are typically prescribed for chest pain, heart arrhythmias, and other problems related to the circulatory system. However, these medications are also used as an off-label treatment for the physical symptoms of social anxiety and panic disorder. Classical musicians, for instance, might take a beta-blocker to reduce shakiness caused by performance anxiety.

Beta-blockers work by reducing the physiological arousal produced by the body's "fight or flight" response. When under stress, the adrenal glands release increased amounts of epinephrine (adrenaline) and norepinephrine (noradrenaline), which prepare the individual to respond to the threat by increasing heart rate and tightening blood vessels. In the case of anxiety disorders, where the threat is either exaggerated or completely absent, beta-blockers can stop the body from responding to the alarm signals being sent by the adrenal glands by clogging up the sites where adrenaline and noradrenaline typically bind with their receptors. This can help to reduce the heart rate, breathing rate, tremors, sweating, and blushing that are the product of adrenaline and noradrenaline circulating throughout the body.

As compared with SSRIs, beta-blockers have the advantage of providing relief quickly, and unlike benzodiazepines, beta-blockers are not considered addictive. Furthermore, beta-blockers appear to have fewer side effects than benzodiazepines and seem to come with less risk when taken for extended periods of time. However, due to limited high-quality research, there is little evidence to support beta-blockers as a safe and effective treatment for anxiety.

26. Are there treatments other than medication and psychotherapy?

While certain psychiatric medications and psychotherapies are considered the standard approaches to treating anxiety disorders, there are many treatments derived from traditions outside of Western medicine that are purported to reduce anxiety. Most of these treatments, collectively referred to as complementary and alternative medicine (CAM), have not been rigorously studied and therefore have little research to support their effectiveness. Despite the lack of evidence to support their use, research suggests that the use of CAM is widespread. Studies have found that 30 to 43 percent of patients treated in primary care for anxiety use CAM treatments. In fact, a 2001 study found that alternative therapies were used more often than conventional therapies by those who reported having anxiety attacks and severe depression.

It is reasonable that many patients who struggle with anxiety turn to these treatments. Evidence-based treatment can be difficult to find; psychotherapy can be expensive and time-consuming. Furthermore, there is a great deal of disagreement among experts about how treatments should be evaluated, which contributes to a sense of confusion about whether a given therapy is more effective than another.

Scientists have developed various methods for testing the effectiveness of a given treatment. Studies can be designed in ways that provide differing levels of confidence that their findings can be applied by clinicians and their patients. Offering the lowest level of confidence that its results can be generalized to other patients, researchers can do a single case study, in which a single patient's response to an intervention is described in detail. Such research is useful in some instances. However, it would not usually be advisable to base treatment decisions on single cases, since it would be impossible to know whether the intervention was genuinely responsible for the patient's outcome as opposed to some other factor.

Providing the highest level of confidence, scientists use a research design known as the randomized controlled trial (RCT). In an RCT, researchers randomly assign participants to two groups (or more). Group A—known as the "intervention group"—receives the treatment that is under investigation, while Group B—known as the "control group"—does not. Subjects in the control group are usually given a placebo (i.e., a substance or procedure that has no therapeutic effect) or an alternative treatment. By comparing results from these two groups, researchers can determine whether the intervention has an effect.

The size of the sample group is also critical. All things being equal, one can place greater confidence in research that has a larger number of participants, so studies using 10,000 participants provide much more convincing evidence than studies using ten participants. As the number of participants increases, it becomes more likely that whatever random differences exist between participants assigned to each group will cancel themselves out.

Meta-analyses combine the data from many studies (usually RCTs) to provide a larger sample size from which conclusions may be drawn. Individual studies frequently get conflicting results, and if two well-designed studies have opposite findings, it is difficult to determine whether one should be trusted over another. Meta-analyses solve this problem by pooling the results of as many studies as possible, which allows scientists to derive conclusions about a large body of research. Like a meta-analysis, a systematic review tries to make sense of an extensive collection of studies but provides qualitative descriptions of the research instead of the quantitative analysis provided by a meta-analysis.

With this information in mind, the research on alternative treatments is discussed later in the chapter.

HERBAL REMEDIES

A 2008 review of research on alternative treatments indicated that there is good evidence that kava, which is made from the root of a plant called *Piper methysticum*, is effective in reducing anxiety. Kava is, however, not currently recommended because it may be toxic to the liver. Inositol, which is naturally found in certain foods, has been found to reduce anxiety in several studies, though it is not currently recommended due to lack of longer-term trials. Passionflower and valerian have also been studied, but neither has been shown to be effective in reducing anxiety. Other herbal remedies that have not been supported by the available research include Bach flower, berocca, ginger, gotu kola, lemongrass leaves, licorice, magnesium, ascorbic acid, and St. John's wort (though there is evidence suggesting that St. John's wort may be helpful for depression). Homeopathic treatments are also not supported by evidence.

DIETARY SUPPLEMENTS

Deficient levels of specific nutrients have been associated with anxiety disorders or with heightened anxiety. Zinc deficiencies, for example, are associated with obsessive-compulsive disorder (OCD) and panic disorder, and vitamin B6 deficiency has been linked to elevated levels of anxiety. Some studies have found that treatments that incorporate certain dietary supplements may lead to improvements in particular anxiety disorders. For example, one small study found that people with OCD who were treated with an SSRI and a zinc supplement for eight weeks showed greater improvements in OCD than those who took only the SSRI and a placebo. Experts do not yet recommend that patients take these supplements, but they consider the early results promising.

AROMATHERAPY

Aromatherapy, which involves the use of fragrances to promote physical or psychological health, has been applied to the treatment of anxiety. A 2011 systematic review determined that aromatherapy seemed to be beneficial in reducing anxiety in patients with dementia receiving palliative care and in patients with cancer. A recent study also found that patients treated in dental offices that had the scent of lavender oil reported lower anxiety than patients treated in offices without this aroma.

EXERCISE

Exercise is physical activity aimed at improving one's strength and/or cardiovascular fitness. High anxiety is a risk factor for a variety of health complications, particularly cardiovascular issues. People with cardiovascular problems who also have high levels of anxiety are more likely to die at an earlier age. It is reasonable to encourage anxious people to exercise more often in the hopes that it will improve their health outcomes, but can exercise be used as a treatment for anxiety?

Several studies have shown that anxiety disorders are less prevalent among those who exercise regularly than among those who do not. This finding, however, does not prove that exercise causes reduced anxiety since it is possible that people with anxiety may not enjoy exercise as much as people who do not suffer from anxiety. Other studies have found that people who do not have anxiety disorders report lower levels of anxiety immediately after exercising, but such studies do not demonstrate that exercise produces any lasting change on anxiety, nor do they prove that exercise reduces anxiety among those who *do* have anxiety disorders.

A systematic review carried out in 2015 suggested that exercise might be a helpful treatment for anxiety disorders, but that because the studies in this area had significant methodological problems, it was not possible to draw firm conclusions about the effectiveness of exercise as a treatment for anxiety. Nonetheless, many studies demonstrate the effectiveness of exercise in reducing anxiety among those who do not have anxiety disorders. Experts, therefore, suggest that exercise may be used as a primary treatment for people who have low levels of anxiety but should not be considered a substitute for medication or psychotherapy among those who have been diagnosed with anxiety disorders.

YOGA

Yoga refers to a group of practices that combine mindful awareness with particular physical activities, which may include holding poses, breathing exercises, and relaxation. Several studies lend support to the idea that yoga practice can lead to reductions in anxiety. However, many of these studies suffered from significant limitations that reduce their usefulness to clinicians and their patients. For example, almost all studies did not use participants who had anxiety disorders, so it is not possible to determine whether yoga is helpful for those with clinically significant anxiety or for those with particular psychiatric conditions.

ACUPUNCTURE

Acupuncture, which is a component of traditional Chinese medicine that involves inserting needles into specific areas of the body, has some research support as a treatment for anxiety. A 2007 study, for example, compared the effectiveness of acupuncture versus a CBT group in the treatment of post-traumatic stress disorder. The results indicated that both groups experienced similar improvements and that both outperformed wait list controls. While these results are encouraging, there were several limitations in the research design, meaning that more studies are needed before firm conclusions can be drawn.

SURGICAL INTERVENTIONS

In extreme cases of OCD that have been resistant to standard treatments, patients may undergo a type of surgery called cingulotomy, in which neurosurgeons, using an electrode or gamma knife, destroy tissue in the cingulate cortex. This area of the brain is thought to be involved in integrating emotions and thoughts and is responsible for directing the brain's attention toward a task. Researchers have found that this surgical procedure led to significant and durable improvement in OCD.

Another surgical procedure that is gaining increased research support is known as deep brain stimulation (DBS). Like cingulotomy, DBS has been used to treat severe OCD that could not be managed using typical methods. In DBS, electrodes are implanted in specific areas of the brain. These electrodes are connected to a device that surgeons implant under the patient's collarbone. Similar to how a pacemaker works on the heart, this device delivers electric pulses to the electrodes in the patient's brain. Early evidence suggests that DBS and cingulotomy yield similar results for patients, but DBS may be preferable because it does not require the destruction of brain tissue.

27. Is it best for people to avoid the things that make them anxious?

Due to countless, incremental improvements across our evolutionary history, humans are equipped with a robust system for detecting and responding to danger. The discomfort that accompanies intense fear is adaptive; just like physical pain, the urgent distress generated by fear compels us to direct our full attention to the problem at hand. By redirecting our attentional resources to the source of danger, the emotion of fear prepares us to mobilize a response, thereby increasing our odds of survival. If the urge to escape is an adaptive response to danger, then shouldn't people heed their internal alarms and escape situations that elicit fear? Would it not be wise to avoid situations that generate anxiety?

While it is adaptive for people to avoid situations that are genuinely threatening, in the modern world, much of what makes us anxious is not imminently hazardous, nor is it likely to be dangerous in the future. In most cases when people act on their urges to avoid, they are responding to dangers that exist only in their imaginations. People who suffer from social anxiety disorder, for example, experience intense fear in social situations and tend to avoid conditions in which they may be evaluated negatively by others. Avoidance of such situations comes at the cost of many meaningful and rewarding experiences and can cause loneliness and depression. The harm caused by social avoidance is especially tragic when one considers that even in the most humiliating situations that the anxiety sufferer can imagine, the risk his or her safety is basically nonexistent. Extremely unpleasant? Yes. Dangerous? Almost definitely not.

Beyond the simple cost of missed opportunities, avoidance also leads people into a downward spiral that increases the likelihood of future difficulties. Someone with panic disorder might worry that he or she will suffer a panic attack while driving to work. Rather than risk this possibility, he or she starts working from home and thereby avoids the anxiety-provoking situation. After deciding to stop driving, the person experiences great relief, which makes it more likely that in the future, he or she will respond to similar situations with fear and avoidance. The individual loses the opportunity to test the accuracy of his or her predictions, making it impossible to disconfirm the belief that driving will elicit panic.

As this cycle continues, the fear may begin to generalize to an increasingly wide range of activities, making the list of avoided situations grow over time. In this way, avoidance, which arises as a solution to the problem of anxiety, eventually becomes the more significant problem as it maintains and strengthens the cycle of anxious avoidance. Once avoidant responses become deeply entrenched, people may find themselves avoiding things that bear little resemblance to the situation that evoked the initial fear. Someone who developed post-traumatic stress disorder after a rape, for example, might start out avoiding the neighborhood where the event occurred, but his or her avoidance could soon spread to larger and larger geographic areas, buildings that resemble the site of the attack, and clothing that reminds him or her of what the attacker was wearing.

28. What do mental health professionals recommend people to do during a panic attack?

Experts suggest that people who experience symptoms of panic get a thorough evaluation, which will determine whether they have panic disorder, some other psychiatric condition, or an underlying medical issue. Assuming that an assessment concludes that the symptoms are not due to a medical problem, there are some strategies that mental health professionals typically recommend to help people cope with the experience.

First, experts agree that it is vital for people to set realistic expectations. Once a panic attack begins, even the most skillful response is unlikely to stop the episode entirely. Professionals, therefore, suggest that people accept that they are likely to experience some discomfort as they navigate a panic event. Consequently, the purpose of applying strategies is not to silence panic symptoms altogether, but rather to turn down the volume. People can expect these techniques to help them reduce their fear so that they can "ride out" their panic and should not expect to terminate an episode immediately.

Second, there is broad consensus that people suffering from panic should become better informed on the topic. Obviously, this learning would have to happen before the onset of a panic attack, since people find it difficult to concentrate and take in new information while experiencing an episode. Being educated about the symptoms of panic, for example, helps people recognize that dizziness and heart palpitations are indications of anxiety and do not signal a threat to their physical safety. Similarly, learning that even though panic attacks feel dangerous and never-ending, they are not life-threatening and will dissipate even if the individual does nothing at all can help people challenge the thought that they are going to die or "go crazy."

Third, experts recommend that people develop an array of coping skills to help them manage their symptoms. As an individual becomes more aware of the typical signs of panic, he or she can intervene earlier in the progression of an episode and use relaxation techniques, breathing exercises, cognitive strategies, or distraction to either avert the attack entirely or at least make it more tolerable. Relaxation techniques may include progressive muscle relaxation, deep breathing, and mindfulness strategies.

Cognitive strategies involve recognizing and challenging distorted and unhelpful thoughts. People may also benefit from grounding techniques, which aim to reduce dissociation and catastrophic thoughts by redirecting the mind toward the present moment.

Therapists—particularly those coming from a cognitive-behavioral background—also advise people not to leave the situation that is evoking the panic attack. Of course, if someone is experiencing blurred vision while driving a car, it is sensible for him or her to pull over and wait for the panic to pass. However, panic attacks do not usually place an individual in any immediate danger. By exiting the situation prematurely, someone may inadvertently condition himself or herself to rely on escape as his or her primary method of managing panic and may inadvertently reinforce the idea that panic attacks are genuinely threatening.

Experts often suggest that family members and friends of those who suffer from panic should also learn more about the symptoms so that—like those who are experiencing the episodes themselves—they can recognize early signs and provide useful feedback. If someone has been diagnosed with panic disorder, friends and family members can help by reminding the individual that he or she is having a panic attack (and not a heart attack), that it is not dangerous, and that it will pass. It is essential for this message to be delivered calmly, patiently, and compassionately, as the panic sufferer may find it difficult to intellectually comprehend or emotionally "take in" this information. The sufferer may also benefit from a reminder to use relaxation strategies or cognitive skills to manage panic.

While some friends and family members may be prone to pressuring someone with panic disorder to expose himself or herself to a level of anxiety that the person is not yet able to tolerate, it is also problematic if friends and family members become overly protective. People may encourage avoidance of distressing situations (e.g., "you had a panic attack the last time you went to school, so you should stay home this week"). They may follow the individual's anxiety-based rules (e.g., avoid disagreeing with one another in the presence of someone who finds conflict anxiety-provoking). They may also behave in ways that reduce the panic sufferer's opportunity to learn new skills (e.g., a friend who provides excessive reassurance that a panic sufferer will not have another panic attack, which impairs his or her ability to predict and plan for future panic attacks realistically).

History and Culture

29. How have the concepts of anxiety and anxiety disorders evolved over time?

The term "anxiety" first appeared in the writings of Sir Thomas More in 1522 and is derived from the Latin word *angere*, which means to strangle or choke. Depictions of anxiety date back 2,500 years to the Greek physician Hippocrates, who described patients with symptoms, such as social avoidance and fear of certain objects, that are immediately recognizable today as reflections of anxiety. The most striking changes in conceptions of anxiety across history come not in the symptoms themselves, which have been largely consistent, but in how the symptoms are explained, categorized, and interpreted.

What follows is a brief review of the way in which humans' understanding of mental illness—particularly anxiety—has developed from the biblical era to the 21st century. For the sake of brevity, this discussion will focus more heavily on developments in Western civilization because they had the most significant impact on Western approaches to anxiety and will place greater emphasis on psychological versus biomedical theories of anxiety.

BIBLICAL ERA THROUGH THE END OF THE ANCIENT GREEK ARCHAIC PERIOD

During the centuries spanning the events depicted in the Old Testament (c. 2000 BCE) until the end of the Archaic period of ancient Greece (c. 500 BCE), madness was understood to be caused by supernatural forces. In the Old Testament, for example, God punished Saul (c. 1082–1010 BCE) by sending an "evil spirit" that "terrified him" (1 Samuel 16:14–23), and which led to paranoia and unpredictable behavior. Contemporary scholars have suggested that Saul may have suffered from depression or mania, but at the time his actions were explained by evil spirits who were sent as a punishment for a moral failure.

CLASSICAL GREECE THROUGH THE FALL OF THE ROMAN EMPIRE

During the years spanning the Classical Greek period (c. 500 BCE) through the fall of the Roman Empire (476 CE), there was a shift from seeing madness as a divine punishment to viewing it as a biological condition. Prior to the Classical period, Greek mythology attributed madness to the actions of gods and goddesses who made people behave abnormally. Mania, a Greek goddess, was often blamed for causing temporary bouts of bizarre behavior. Another god, Pan (from whose name the modern word "panic" is derived), was believed to arouse terror in people. Mental health treatment was provided by priests using prayers, sacrifices, and dream interpretation.

The Greek physician Hippocrates (c. 460–357 BCE) challenged these theories, proposing that illnesses—including mental illnesses—were caused by biology and not supernatural forces. Greek medicine, as refined and systematized by Hippocrates, was based on the belief that disease resulted from an imbalance among four basic bodily fluids, or "humors" (yellow bile, black bile, phlegm, and blood), which were contained in the human body. After determining whether the patient had a deficiency or an excess in a particular humor, the doctor would attempt to correct this imbalance. Bloodletting, for instance, was a treatment that sought to restore the body's equilibrium by draining a quantity of blood.

Hippocrates provided the earliest known depiction of a specific phobia when, in 400 BCE, he described a man who would be "beset by terror" upon hearing "the first note of the flute at a banquet." Furthermore, Hippocrates delineated a condition called *melancholia*, which he attributed to an excess of "black bile." Melancholia was characterized by "fears and dependencies, if they last a long time," and included symptoms of emotional distress that modern psychiatrists would separate into the categories of depressive disorders and anxiety disorders.

Roman philosophers offered insights into anxiety that are largely consistent with modern ideas. For example, Cicero (106–43 BCE) distinguished between "trait" anxiety (*anxietas*) and the more transient "state" anxiety (*angor*), and also made a distinction between anxiety (*angor*) and worry (*sollicitudo*). Anticipating the existentialist philosophy of the 19th and 20th centuries, Seneca (4 BCE–65 CE) suggested that anxiety about mortality is the main impediment to enjoying life. Seneca proposed that the best way to reduce anxiety is to focus on the present moment and to avoid ruminating on the past or worrying about the future, which is similar to current techniques of mindfulness meditation. About 2,000 years before cognitive therapy would recognize the role of faulty cognitions in generating emotional distress, Seneca wrote that "there are more things to alarm us than to harm us, and we suffer more in apprehension than in reality."

THE FALL OF ROME TO THE 17TH CENTURY

With the ascendance of the Christian church, the period from the fall of Rome in 476 CE through the 17th century witnessed a return to religious explanations for madness. During much of this period, madness was interpreted as a sign of sin or possession by evil spirits, and the mentally ill were often treated brutally. Hippocrates's naturalistic theory of illness was replaced with the doctrine of the Christian church, which taught that madness was the result of sin, a curse, or demonic possession. The evil forces that caused abnormal behavior were believed to be contagious, and treatment could consist of exorcism, torture, or execution.

Although the biological theory of illness was lost in Western Europe after the fall of the Roman Empire, it was absorbed by the Muslim world, where it flourished. In contrast to the brutal treatment of the mentally ill emanating from Church doctrine, the Koran did not ascribe mental illness to demons or sin and advised humane treatment of the mentally ill. Diagnostic categories for anxiety disorders were developed by the Muslim physician Unhammad (870–925 CE), whose description of what he labeled *murrae souda* is strikingly similar to what we now classify as obsessive-compulsive disorder. Humoral theory was reintroduced to the West in the 10th and 11th centuries through interactions between Muslim culture and the West.

17TH AND 18TH CENTURIES

Beginning in the 17th century, there was a return to the notion that mental illnesses were caused by faulty biology and not by sin or spiritual decay. Doctors began to see illness as the result of disturbances in the brain and nervous system. Physicians, such as Thomas Sydenham (1624–1689), sought to approach the study of diseases using observation and data collection rather than speculation. Sydenham proposed that every disease had a typical way of presenting itself across individuals. This contrasted with the Hippocratic notion of melancholia, in which a single condition could be expressed in vastly different ways depending on the individual.

Driven by technological innovation, the Industrial Revolution that began in the 18th century led to rapid societal changes across the United States and much of Europe. The unprecedented rate of change brought greater prosperity but also overturned social structures on which people had previously relied. Increasing belief in the value of science and medicine among the upper class, in combination with feelings of uncertainty wrought by social upheaval, paved the way for growing interest in the treatment of anxiety as a medical problem.

In 1733, George Cheyne (1671–1743) published *The English Malady*, which popularized the idea that disturbances in the nervous system were responsible for a category of conditions he called "nervous distempers," which included hypochondria, melancholia, and hysteria. At that time, the word "nervous" meant "pertaining to the nerves" and did not refer to the subjective experience of "feeling nervous" as it is currently used. Cheyne proposed that the incidence of these illnesses was exploding due to the rapid cultural shifts occurring in 18th-century England. His assertion that these conditions were a result of prosperity and civilization helped nervous disorders to become a fashionable sign of social status among the wealthy.

Treatise on Madness, published in 1758 by William Battie (1703–1776), was the first work to present anxiety as a distinct mental disorder. Battie believed that anxiety was caused by problems with the nervous system. Like other physicians of his day, Battie distinguished anxiety from the severe mental illnesses that were referred to as "madness." During the 18th and 19th centuries, madness was treated in hospitals by psychiatrists, while nervous disorders were treated by general physicians. As nervous conditions grew in popularity, a new specialty of "nerve doctors" emerged to treat the predominately affluent and female clientele who sought help for these nervous conditions.

19TH CENTURY

Charles Darwin's theory of evolution, which proposed that emotions such as fear were innate, further reinforced the notion that anxiety (and by extension the nervous disorders resulting from anxiety) had a biological origin. Continuing the trend toward medicalization that began in the 18th century, 19th-century physicians considered mental illness a physical problem that was linked to the workings of the nervous system. Symptoms of anxiety were explained as disturbances in the nerves, brain, cardiovascular system, or inner ear.

Medicine required new terms to describe the various nervous conditions that were being identified. In 1869, the American neurologist George Miller Beard popularized the diagnosis of "neurasthenia" (literally translated as "tired nerves"), which could be applied to a vast set of symptoms, including fatigue, anxiety, and sexual dysfunction. Beard suggested that neurasthenia was a uniquely American affliction that disproportionately affected people who were highly civilized (by which he meant those with wealth and social status). Though neurasthenia was defined so vaguely as to be nearly meaningless, it became a popular diagnosis because it provided patients with an explanation for their symptoms that was rooted in biology, which carried less stigma than having a mental illness.

20TH CENTURY

Until the late 19th century, the physical manifestations of anxiety were treated as though they were typical medical illnesses. A patient with symptoms of panic, for instance, might be sent to a heart specialist to treat chest pain, a gastric specialist to treat digestive symptoms, and an inner ear specialist to treat dizziness. At the same time, physicians, perhaps reacting against the vagueness of neurasthenia as a diagnosis, began to propose new diagnoses to categorize the symptoms encompassed by neurasthenia.

The work of Sigmund Freud (1856–1939), a Viennese neurologist, brought about a radical shift in conceptions of mental illness. Whereas biological theories had dominated the field since the 18th century, Freud emphasized the role of internal mental processes (i.e., psychology) in the development of emotional disturbances. Prior to Freud, anxiety was considered a symptom of other disorders and had therefore been given little consideration. In Freudian theory, by contrast, anxiety was centrally important. In an 1894 paper, Freud proposed that anxiety disorders represented a distinct diagnostic category and argued that anxiety was at the core of several different syndromes, such as anxiety attacks, generalized anxiety, phobias, and obsessions. Anxiety quickly replaced neurasthenia as the primary explanation for the so-called neurotic disorders.

Freud's perspective on anxiety changed over the course of his career, so for the sake of clarity, this review will focus on his final formulation. Freud conceptualized the psyche as being made up of three parts: the *id*, which contains our sexual and aggressive impulses and seeks immediate gratification; the *superego*, which internalizes social rules and can be thought of as our "conscience"; and the *ego*, which is the conscious self. The *ego* is responsible for navigating external reality and must balance the conflicting desires of the *id* and *superego*. The workings of the *ego* are sometimes accessible to the conscious mind, whereas the *id* and *superego* operate outside of conscious awareness.

In his later writings, Freud regarded the conscious experience of anxiety as a signal generated by the unconscious mind as a warning of impending danger to the psyche. This danger could result from a conflict between the urges of the *id*, which might seek to behave in a manner that violates the morality of the *superego*. Although the individual may not be able to consciously pinpoint the source of the conflict, anxiety triggers the unconscious deployment of a defense mechanism to avoid distress. One of the most fundamental of these defense mechanisms is *repression*, in which the ego forces unacceptable thoughts, memories, or urges into the unconscious. Freud suggested that *neuroses* (meaning anxiety disorders) were the result of urges that had been repressed, but which continued to exert pressure by creating internal conflict. Freudian *psychoanalysis* attempted to restore balance to the relationship among the id, ego, and superego by helping the patient consciously access and resolve the repressed conflicts that were responsible for the anxiety.

The popularity of psychoanalysis began to wane starting in the late 1960s. One of the main reasons for the decline was the growing popularity of newly introduced psychiatric medications, which reduced the demand and necessity for psychoanalysis. Medications were inexpensive, accessible, and provided quick relief from symptoms, whereas psychoanalysis was costly, time-consuming, and could require multiple sessions per week for years before the patient experienced relief.

In addition to competition resulting from the advent of psychiatric medication for anxiety, psychoanalysis was challenged by the development of treatment for anxiety based on behavioral theories. During World War II, psychologists using behavioral approaches were called upon to teach soldiers to manage their fear during combat. Psychologists developed effective strategies that could be communicated quickly, and the speed of behaviorism as an agent of change made it more attractive to people who sought rapid improvement after the war ended.

Behaviorism, which was developed in part by John Watson (1878–1958) and B. F. Skinner (1904–1990), proposed that people were not motivated by unconscious conflicts or innate drives, but rather that people reacted to their environments based on past learning. If a given behavior led to positive consequences in the past, the behavior would increase, and if the behavior was ignored or led to aversive consequences, the behavior would be reduced.

In this view, anxiety disorders developed because the individual had been reinforced for maladaptive behaviors (i.e., avoidance). Consequently, the individual's anxiety could be treated by changing the consequences of his or her behavior. Unlike psychoanalysis, which focused on unconscious processes that were unobservable, behaviorists focused only on actions that were observable and quantifiable. Whereas psychoanalysts were interested in generating insight, behaviorists considered measurable symptomatic improvement the only relevant goal. One prominent form of behavioral therapy for anxiety, known as systematic desensitization, involved teaching patients relaxation strategies (e.g., deep breathing), which the patients would apply at the same time they were gradually being exposed to a feared situation.

Behaviorism fell out of favor in the late 20th century due to research findings that conflicted with some of its assumptions. For example, researchers demonstrated that some fears were more easily triggered than others, indicating a genetic basis. This conflicted with behaviorism, which assumed that all fears were learned and strengthened through interactions with the external world. Furthermore, research on temperament showed that fearful infants tended to grow up to be more fearful adults, which similarly challenged the behaviorist notion that people are controlled purely by reinforcement provided by the environment.

Behaviorism was complemented by cognitive approaches to anxiety, which emphasized the role of faulty cognitions in generating pathological anxiety. Cognitive therapy, which focuses on modifying maladaptive thoughts and beliefs, was first developed by Aaron T. Beck (1921–). Beginning in the early 1960s, Beck focused on the role of faulty information processing in anxiety and depression. Beck's cognitive therapy sought to treat anxiety and depression by targeting what he called the "negative cognitive triad," which were negative beliefs that patients had regarding the self (e.g., "I am weak"), the world (e.g., "the world is dangerous," "I can't trust anyone"), and the future (e.g., "things will never get better").

From the 1980s through today, there has been a shift toward integrating concepts drawn from the cognitive and behavioral traditions. Treatments that are based on the combination of these ideas are collectively known as cognitive-behavioral therapy (CBT), which remains the dominant psychological approach to understanding and treating anxiety.

The ascendance of CBT coincided with the growth of the biomedical model of anxiety. While psychological approaches view anxiety disorders as the product of cognition and experience, biomedical approaches see anxiety disorders as a physical problem rooted in the brain. With the development of a variety of medications for anxiety disorders, as well as exciting new research on the brain regions, neurotransmitters, and genes that are associated with anxiety, the biomedical model has once again become the dominant approach to understanding anxiety.

From the time of Hippocrates to the present, humanity's conception of anxiety has been characterized by dueling perspectives. Are anxiety disorders a physical problem, rooted in an imbalance among the four humors, dysfunction in the nerves, or faulty genes? Or are anxiety disorders caused by moral weakness, unconscious conflict, reinforcement of maladaptive behavior, or flawed thinking? The pendulum has swung back and forth throughout the history of Western civilization, and a definitive answer has yet to emerge.

30. How does culture impact anxiety?

This is a complex and thought-provoking topic. The *Diagnostic and Statistical Manual of Mental Disorders* (DSM) and the philosophy underlying its conception of mental health are based upon Western medical concepts. The DSM, therefore, represents a Western perspective on what constitutes an illness, what causes the illness, and in whom the illness is thought to reside. It is therefore important to ask whether the anxiety disorders that are delineated in the DSM (and indeed all psychiatric diagnoses) are universally applicable, or whether they are useful only in a particular time and geographic area, namely modern Western countries. Given that approximately 75 percent of the human population is non-Western, and that our conceptualization of mental illness has changed dramatically over the past century, it is reasonable to question the relevance of these diagnoses to other cultures.

Maintaining our focus on anxiety disorders, those who view anxiety as a biomedical problem might argue that since the human body has not changed significantly for the past several thousand years and shows little variation across cultures, anxiety should therefore exist across time and cultural context. In this view, culture can only influence the way that anxiety is interpreted and expressed, but not the underlying biological mechanisms that give rise to the experience. The diagnosis of obsessive-compulsive disorder (OCD) provides a useful illustration of how a psychiatric disorder can be expressed in various cultures. Because all human brains are comprised of the same biological structures, it is reasonable to suggest that all cultures should have some number of people who struggle to control their thoughts and are compelled to act on urges.

Research does, in fact, suggest that OCD exists across cultures. However, each culture, with its own unique set of beliefs and fears, differs in the content of the obsessive thoughts and in the types of compulsive behaviors that are most common. One study, for instance, found that highly religious Western Christians with OCD most often reported obsessions regarding the importance of controlling one's thoughts, which is consistent with the notion—common in certain strains of Christianity—that thinking about committing a sin is the moral equivalent of engaging in the sinful behavior.

Experts hypothesize that because Judaism requires adherence to a complex and exacting system of laws, highly observant Jews with OCD are likely to experience anxiety about whether they have been sufficiently careful about completing their religious rituals and they often fear divine punishment for potential errors. Practitioners of Orthodox Judaism are expected to follow a complicated set of rules that govern many behaviors. There is a set of 39 laws about what one may and may not do on the Sabbath. There are multiple prayers to be said before and after meals, during travels, after certain natural phenomena, and so on. There are laws that govern business practices, eating, and interactions between men and women. Given the sheer number of laws, it is reasonable that OCD among Orthodox Jews would often center around rigidly following these rules.

Among Muslims, researchers studying OCD in Turkey found that obsessions frequently centered around fears of contamination and concern for cleanliness, which they attributed to the Islamic focus on rituals, purity, and cleanliness. Research on a small sample of women from Saudi Arabia with OCD found that some of the women reported a belief that their OCD was caused by the "evil eye," which is a curse brought about by a malevolent stare. Research on OCD in Pakistan, where Islam is the dominant religion, found that the most common compulsion was handwashing, while the most common obsessions involved fear of germs. These researchers suggested that this is consistent with a concept in Islamic culture known as

"Napak," which is a feeling of being unclean or unholy and which requires an individual to cleanse himself or herself before engaging in religious rituals such as prayer or reading from the Koran.

In Bali, where Hinduism is the dominant religion, a study on a small sample of OCD sufferers found a high incidence of the "need to know obsession," which, in the study participants, was experienced as the obsessive need to know the identities of passersby. This study also found that consistent with religious beliefs in Bali, those with OCD reported obsessions involving ghosts, magic, and witchcraft.

Beyond religious differences, research has also indicated that there are differences in the way OCD is expressed depending on geographical region. For example, a study of people with OCD in Rio de Janeiro, Brazil, found aggressive obsessions to be most common, followed by obsessions regarding contamination, while a study on those with OCD in Mexico found contamination obsessions to be most common, followed by sexual obsessions and aggressive obsessions. A study on people in Japan with OCD found contamination obsessions to be most common, followed by obsessions regarding symmetry and obsessions involving aggression. A study on OCD in a Chinese sample found obsessions involving symmetry to be most common, followed by fears of contamination and obsessions related to aggression.

As is the case with OCD, panic attacks share a core set of features across different cultures, which involve the sudden onset of physiological symptoms and catastrophic interpretations of what these symptoms mean. Just as the cultural context influences the thought content on which the OCD sufferer becomes fixated, culture also plays a part in determining which symptoms of a panic attack are experienced as most distressing. One dramatic example of this occurs among Cambodian refugees, who have reported feelings of terror if they experience dizziness after standing up. This fear makes sense when one considers the common Cambodian belief that, like blood, there is a "wind" (*khyâl*) that circulates through the body. Upon experiencing somatic symptoms of anxiety, a Cambodian might interpret his or her discomfort as a malfunction in the flow of wind, which leads to fear of imminent harm. When a Cambodian with these beliefs feels dizzy upon standing up, he or she may see this as an indication of a "wind attack" (*gaeut khyâl*), which, if not treated through a ritualized behavior aimed at removing the wind, could lead to death.

To those raised outside of this cultural context, Cambodian beliefs about wind may seem strange. However, this example illustrates the way in which an individual's culture provides the language and the conceptual framework though which his or her emotional distress is understood, communicated, and treated by the individual and larger community.

❖

Case Studies

CASE 1: ANNA—SPECIFIC PHOBIA

Anna was a ten-year-old girl who came to therapy due to an extreme fear of vomiting, which developed in the aftermath of a bad case of the flu. A few weeks after getting over the flu, Anna's teacher told her parents that Anna seemed more reserved and distant from her peers. At her parent–teacher conference a couple of months later, the teacher said that Anna had been asking to go to the nurse for a variety of ailments (many of which the teacher believed were fabricated), was not eating lunch because she said all the food made her nauseated, and had requested to move to a seat near the door "in case I need to throw up." Her parents also noticed that Anna kept asking them if they were feeling well. If her parents coughed or sneezed, Anna would move to the opposite side of the room and would instruct them to wash their hands before hugging her goodnight.

Anna's teacher also noticed that she seemed to be having trouble with concentration. When the teacher suggested that Anna move back to her old seat in the front row, Anna became uncharacteristically angry and stormed out of the classroom. Anna refused to go to school the next day. After a particularly intense argument, her parents agreed to let her stay home from school if she promised that she would go the next day without disagreement. Anna accepted their offer but then didn't go to school for the next two weeks. Anna's parents were only successful in getting her to return by threatening to give away her cat. They used this same threat to get her to see a therapist since this was the only way they could motivate her to go to an unfamiliar place.

Using her sleeve to prevent contact with the doorknob, Anna entered the therapist's office timidly and sat close to the door. When asked why she had done this, Anna replied that she felt sick and might need to leave quickly. After speaking with Anna, her parents, teachers, and her pediatrician, the therapist diagnosed Anna with a specific phobia. Anna's condition, he explained, was called emetophobia—an extreme and irrational fear of vomiting. The therapist described how he, as a cognitive-behavioral therapist, would approach Anna's treatment using a combination of cognitive restructuring and exposure.

Anna met with her therapist weekly, and early sessions focused on helping Anna recognize the physical sensations that accompany her emotions. This allowed Anna to learn that anxiety almost always preceded her nausea. Anna identified her internal and external triggers for anxiety, and this awareness made her nausea feel more predictable. Therapy then moved on to cognitive restructuring, in which Anna was first taught to see the relationship between her thoughts (e.g., "I'm going to throw up if I eat in the lunchroom") and her emotional responses (anxiety and fear). Anna learned to discern and then challenge the cognitive distortions that were making her so confident that she would vomit. For example, Anna identified the cognitive distortion called "generalization," which led her to assume that because she became nauseated and vomited when she had the flu, this proved that she would vomit every time she experienced nausea in the future. To challenge this thought, Anna reminded herself that even though she feared vomiting many times per day, this had in fact not happened once since she had the flu months earlier.

Anna now felt prepared to begin exposing herself to situations and objects that elicited nausea. Exposure, she was told, would teach her to tolerate her distress without avoidance and would help her learn that feeling nauseated would not lead to catastrophic consequences. Anna and her therapist developed a hierarchy of feared situations. Lower-level items included talking about vomiting, medium items included watching a video of someone vomiting, and the highest items included hugging family members when they had recently been sick. Anna was assigned daily exposure tasks, and as she made her way up the hierarchy, she noticed that it became easier and easier to complete the exposures. After four months of therapy, Anna, her therapist, and her parents agreed that she was ready to stop treatment.

Analysis

The term used to describe a specific phobia of vomiting is *emetophobia.* People with emetophobia are often surprised to learn that their problem has a name and that effective treatments are available. Emetophobes often develop a wide range of avoidance behaviors to prevent themselves from becoming nauseated or being exposed to vomit. They may stop eating foods that they deem likely to cause nausea, and in extreme cases, emetophobes may restrict eating to such an extent that professionals mistakenly diagnose them with anorexia.

Compared with other forms of anxiety, there has been relatively little research on emetophobia, so there is limited information on how the disorder arises, how the disorder tends to behave over time, or how it is best treated. However, there is some evidence that—as illustrated in Anna's case—emetophobia often starts in childhood after the individual vomits or observes someone else vomiting.

From the perspective of a cognitive-behavioral therapist, the reason why someone develops a phobia is less important than how the fear is developed and maintained. Whatever its original cause, Anna had gotten stuck in the following cycle of thoughts, emotions, and behaviors:

- Anna would experience an internal trigger (i.e., a thought or physical sensation) or an external trigger (e.g., watching a television show in which a character got sick).
- She would inaccurately evaluate the trigger as threatening and might think, for example, that seeing someone get sick on television would imminently cause her to vomit.
- Her interpretation of the trigger as dangerous would lead to high levels of fear.
- Anna would act in accordance with her mistaken beliefs, meaning that she would escape or avoid situations that triggered anxiety-related thoughts, emotions, and physical sensations (e.g., she would turn off the television and would not watch that show again).

Anna's fear became problematic when she began to act in ways (i.e., avoidance behaviors) that were consistent with her inaccurate belief that nausea was dangerous. Once she became reliant on avoidance as her primary method of coping, she lost the opportunity to correct the beliefs that were making her avoid the experience of nausea. Exposure therapy provided Anna the chance to learn that the internal and external triggers for anxiety that she had been avoiding would probably not make her vomit, and that she could tolerate nausea without actually vomiting.

CASE 2: OLIVIA AND MADELINE—PANIC DISORDER

Olivia and Madeline, both in their early 30s, have been coworkers for the past several years. Until the topic came up recently by chance, neither knew that the other also suffered from panic disorder. They began to compare their experiences and realized that they shared several features in common: they were diagnosed at around the same age (early 20s), they first learned of panic disorder after going to the emergency room due to fearing a heart attack, and they both had family members with anxiety disorders. They also noted that although they had the same diagnosis and experienced similar panic symptoms, the treatment they received had been drastically different.

Olivia explained that following her emergency room visit, she was given a referral for a cognitive-behavioral therapist at a clinic near her home. The therapist spoke with Olivia's general physician, who ran some tests and confirmed that Olivia didn't have any medical disorders that could explain her symptoms. Olivia and her psychologist decided that in addition to receiving cognitive-behavioral therapy (CBT), she would benefit from medications. Her psychologist referred to a psychiatrist, who prescribed fluoxetine (Prozac).

In CBT, Olivia was provided with information on the nature of anxiety and panic attacks. She learned about the connection between her physical sensations, her catastrophic interpretations of these sensations, and her avoidance behaviors, and how these responses created a feedback loop that perpetuated her panic attacks. Olivia's therapist taught her to reduce her physiological arousal by controlling her breathing and showed her how to modify the thoughts that were generating anxiety. For example, she learned how to challenge the thought "I'm going to have a heart attack," and to replace it with the thought "I have had many panic attacks, and I've never had a heart attack before, so it's improbable that it will happen this time." She practiced exposing herself to situations that she had been avoiding so that she could learn to manage her anxiety more effectively. Through interoceptive exposure tasks inside and outside of therapy sessions, she was able to correct her belief that dizziness and light-headedness are dangerous sensations that she needed to avoid.

Olivia went to therapy for 20 weeks, and noting significant improvement, she and her psychologist decided she was ready to stop meeting for therapy. Olivia discontinued Prozac a few times over the years, but she noticed that her panic attacks became more frequent when she was off the medication. Even on the drug, she still had panic attacks a few times a year, but she found that they were much more tolerable and less disruptive to her life.

Madeline's illness had followed a very different course. Like Olivia, Madeline had been offered a referral for a psychologist after going to the emergency room. Unlike Olivia, Madeline insisted that her symptoms were "real" and not "in her head," so she made an appointment with her general physician to help her identify and treat the "physical" problem. At Madeline's request, her physician referred her to a cardiologist (because Madeline was afraid that the sensations in her chest were a sign of something wrong with her heart), an endocrinologist (because Madeline thought a hormonal imbalance might be the culprit), and a neurologist (because Madeline read that dizziness, weakness, and a tingling sensation in the extremities can be symptoms of a brain tumor). Each specialist listened patiently, administered the appropriate tests, and concluded that Madeline was suffering from panic attacks.

Feeling defeated, Madeline accepted a prescription from her general physician for alprazolam (Xanax). Madeline's doctor instructed her to take 4 milligrams per day but told her that she could take more if she started to feel symptoms of panic and needed quick relief. Up until this point, Madeline had always preferred to avoid taking medications, but she felt so much better on Xanax that she would finish a full month's supply within two weeks, leading her doctor to keep raising the dosage. After three months. Madeline was taking an average of 12 milligrams per day.

Had he done a more thorough evaluation of her psychiatric history, Madeline's doctor would have learned that she struggled with alcoholism in high school and college, which would have made him more cautious about raising her dosage repeatedly. After she finished a month's worth of Xanax in ten days, Madeline's doctor said that he was concerned that she might be getting addicted and refused to write a new prescription. Madeline desperately tried to convince him that she was fine, but he wouldn't budge.

The next day, Madeline went without Xanax for the first time in almost a year and felt anxiety that was more uncomfortable and prolonged than any panic attack she had ever experienced. On the second day, she developed symptoms of what she thought was the flu: a headache, shakiness, vomiting, sweatiness, and achiness across her whole body. Light began to feel painfully bright, and the sound of her phone became intolerably loud. She shut off her phone to avoid the grinding pain generated by every notification. When her mother couldn't reach her for two days, she became alarmed and rushed to Madeline's apartment, where she found her daughter having a seizure on the bathroom floor.

After being rushed to the emergency room, Madeline was medically stabilized and given a longer-acting benzodiazepine to reduce her withdrawal symptoms. Madeline was given a referral for a psychiatrist and psychologist, which she gladly accepted. Madeline's psychiatrist gradually tapered her off the benzodiazepines over the next six months, and with the help of therapy and antidepressant medication, her panic symptoms improved significantly.

Analysis

Madeline and Olivia both represent the "textbook" panic disorder patient: both are female, have family members with anxiety disorders, and had an onset of the condition in their early 20s. Olivia and Madeline were lucky to have been told that they might have panic disorder at their first visit to the emergency room, as one study found that none of the research participants who went to the emergency room due to panic attacks were diagnosed correctly.

This case example illustrates the vast difference between treatment that follows evidence-based clinical guidelines and treatment based on the limited knowledge of a single provider. Olivia's treatment was based on the best available evidence, as research has found that CBT is an effective treatment for panic disorder and that there is some benefit to combining CBT with an antidepressant, such as Prozac.

Madeline's treatment clearly did not follow clinical guidelines. Though it is widely recognized that Xanax can rapidly reduce the symptoms of panic disorder, there is some disagreement among experts as to whether it should be considered a first-line treatment for anxiety disorders. Experts would, however, agree that physicians must assess for a history of substance abuse before prescribing a benzodiazepine, because people who have already struggled with an addiction are more likely than others to become dependent on medications from this class. Experts generally agree that the initial dosage for Xanax should be about 1 milligram total per day and should be increased very gradually. Doses above 6 milligrams per day (which is already quite high) should be considered only after ruling out any medical cause or other life stress, and 12 milligrams per day goes beyond the highest dosage that has been tested in clinical trials.

Madeline's physician made a genuinely grave error in judgment when, after she ran out of the medication, he refused to prescribe more Xanax and sent her away without a plan for how to manage her withdrawal.

As illustrated by Madeline's case, abruptly discontinuing or reducing benzodiazepines—particularly when people have been taking high doses for an extended period—can be fatal. Experts recommend that the dosage of benzodiazepines should be reduced by no more than 10 percent every two weeks to lower the risk of serious withdrawal symptoms.

The single greatest difference between Olivia and Madeline was in their initial response to the suggestion that they had suffered a panic attack. Olivia responded by accepting the recommendation to see a therapist, while Madeline resisted this advice because she felt that it minimized her suffering. Though the stigma surrounding mental illness has lessened in recent years, many people continue to believe that psychological suffering is less "real" than the pain that comes from "physical" sources. There is little logic to this claim since psychological pain emanates from the same body and brain that produce "physical" pain. Given that there are safe and effective treatments for panic disorder, it is tragic that anyone should deny himself or herself relief because of society's confusion on this issue.

CASE 3: CASSIE—COMORBID ANXIETY AND DEPRESSION

Cassie is a 38-year-old woman who sought therapy six months after giving birth to twin daughters. She and her husband had been trying to have a baby for years, and she was elated when she learned that she would be having twins. Cassie's enthusiasm turned to fear when she had to deliver four weeks ahead of schedule because one of the twins was not getting enough oxygen. The babies spent the first several weeks of their lives in the hospital, and though they were perfectly healthy at five months old, Cassie experienced a recurring nightmare in which she looked on helplessly as the smaller twin stopped breathing and turned to smoke.

Cassie was anxious while the babies were in the hospital, but she was hopeful that she'd feel better when they were finally ready to come home. She was surprised to find that her stress only got worse when the babies were discharged from the hospital. Cassie struggled to get them to nap at the same time, which meant that she rarely got more than a couple of hours of uninterrupted sleep per night. She often felt irritable and found herself picking fights with her husband that she immediately regretted. Cassie noticed that she felt anxious nearly all the time and found herself on the verge of tears through much of the day. Her mother and sisters assured her that it was normal for her to be more emotional after giving birth. They encouraged Cassie to relax and enjoy her time with the babies. Cassie's family reminded her that she had overcome her psychological problems in high school and they expressed certainty that she would be fine once she settled into her new role as a mother.

Unfortunately, contrary to the predictions of her family, Cassie's anxiety worsened in the coming weeks. Cassie told her therapist that although she had always been a worrier, these anxious thoughts had become so intense and frequent that she was rarely able to redirect her attention from them for more than a few minutes at a time. Before giving birth, Cassie believed that her tendency to worry had made her a better student, employee, and friend. Always expecting things to go wrong, she made sure to be ready in case of some improbable disaster. The critical difference was that before, Cassie recognized that her predictions were overly pessimistic, and she knew that realistically, things would usually work out. Now, she said, anxiety clouded her thinking in a way that made it difficult for her to distinguish between realistic and unrealistic fears. Was it reasonable for her to worry that her husband died in a car accident because he was 30 minutes late and hadn't called, or was anxiety distorting her assessment of the situation? She did not know, and this uncertainty was hard for her to tolerate.

Cassie's intolerance of uncertainty led her to agonize over small daily decisions, such as what to cook for dinner, when to feed the babies, and how to arrange the furniture in her living room. When choices needed to be made, she felt waves of fear that prevented her from concentrating on the task at hand. To solve this problem, she would call her husband and ask him what she should do. At first, hopeful that she would feel more supported, Cassie's husband was happy to help her weigh the pros and cons of whatever issue was troubling her. Cassie felt such relief during these conversations that she found herself calling him more and more often, and she sometimes called just a few minutes after their last call had ended to double-check that they had reached the right decision. Her husband quickly lost patience, and he abruptly stopped answering her calls during work hours.

Cassie started calling her mother instead, but she proved even less accommodating than her husband. For the first time since high school, Cassie began to get panic attacks. She was overcome with worries about many different issues, and her mind seemed to have a never-ending supply of disconnected thoughts that put her on a path toward panic. "Are the babies developing normally?" "Do people miss me at work?" "Is my husband having an affair?" "Where should the girls go to school?" "Will climate change destroy humanity?"

Her most prominent worry, which she was ashamed to admit aloud, was that she did not love her daughters. After a series of miscarriages and a failed attempt at in vitro fertilization (IVF), Cassie had resigned herself to the fact that she would never have children. She knew that she was incredibly fortunate to have had two beautiful and healthy baby girls, but she couldn't escape the feeling that her life was better without them. She felt no warmth when the babies cried, which she took as evidence that she was an unfit parent and a defective human being.

Cassie took her daughters to the park and watched the other new parents gaze at their babies lovingly. The other parents talked excitedly about their children, made play dates with one another, and appeared to be genuinely happy. Cassie stopped leaving the house except for when the babies needed to see the pediatrician. She had little appetite and noticed with a sense of indifference that she had lost ten pounds in two weeks. When alone, Cassie spent most of her time crying. Though she felt exhausted, she found it difficult to fall asleep.

Cassie had not felt so lonely since her junior year of high school when her anxiety and depression had gotten so bad that she turned to self-injury to manage her distress. Cassie told her husband that she was afraid she was losing her mind and that she had recently started having thoughts about ending her own life. Cassie was surprised when he responded with kindness and concern. Immediately after their conversation, Cassie's husband asked a friend for help finding a therapist and scheduled the initial appointment.

Cassie confessed that she was afraid that the therapist thought she was a terrible person. The therapist responded that she, too, had experienced depression and anxiety after her first child was born and that she suffered from many of the same self-judgments that Cassie described. The therapist explained that Cassie's emotional detachment from her daughters was not a moral failure, but instead that it was a symptom of depression. The therapist expressed confidence that with effort Cassie could expect significant improvement in the next two to three months. Cassie smiled and said she was ready to get to work.

Analysis

After just one session, Cassie's therapist would not have enough information to make a diagnosis, but she would be able to make some strong preliminary guesses. Assuming that all physical causes (e.g., thyroid disease) have been ruled out, there are several potential candidates for Cassie's diagnosis.

Cassie's recurrent nightmares could be a sign of post-traumatic stress disorder (PTSD). A study published in 2017 found that postpartum PTSD is remarkably common, affecting 5 to 8 percent of mothers who were surveyed one to three months after childbirth. The study identified several factors that were associated with increased risk for postpartum PTSD, some of which applied to Cassie, including a history of anxiety that predated the pregnancy, delivery via emergency procedure, premature delivery, and an experience in which the mother feared for the child's safety. However, nightmares are also associated with other anxiety-based conditions, as well as depression, dissociative disorders, and borderline personality disorder. The therapist would have to ask many more questions to determine whether Cassie had PTSD.

Based on her report of multiple recent panic attacks, as well as her history of panic attacks in high school, it seems likely that Cassie has panic disorder. Before making this diagnosis, the therapist would need to collect more information to make sure that the experiences Cassie described as panic attacks matched the diagnostic criteria laid out in the *DSM-5*. Panic attacks are the key characteristic of panic disorder, but they can also accompany social anxiety disorder, PTSD, substance use, specific phobias, obsessive-compulsive disorder, and depression, so the presence of panic attacks would not necessarily indicate that Cassie had panic disorder. Unlike the panic attacks seen in other conditions, a diagnosis of panic disorder requires that at least two of the attacks must be of the "unexpected" type, meaning that these episodes were not triggered by an identifiable stimulus.

It seems very likely that Cassie would be diagnosed with major depressive disorder (MDD). She endorsed many of the symptoms listed in the *DSM-5*, including depressed mood, loss of interest in social interaction, change in appetite and weight, difficulty sleeping, fatigue, excessive feelings of guilt, indecisiveness and concentration problems, and suicidal thoughts. The *DSM-5* allows clinicians to append "specifiers" to certain diagnoses, which offer a bit of additional detail on the patient's condition. For mothers who develop depression during pregnancy or in the first four weeks following birth, a clinician can add the "with peripartum onset" specifier. The previous version of the *DSM* had a specifier for "postpartum onset," but the newer revision changed the specifier to "peripartum onset" due to research showing that about 50 percent of "postpartum" depressive episodes begin *during* pregnancy. According to the *DSM-5*, between 3 and 6 percent of women experience a depressive episode during pregnancy or in the months after they deliver.

Cassie would probably also be diagnosed with generalized anxiety disorder (GAD). She reported multiple symptoms of GAD, which included excessive anxiety and worry that she found difficult to control, fatigue, problems with concentration, irritability, and sleep disturbance. It is considered normal for new parents to worry about the health of their newborns, which can make it difficult to distinguish the normal anxiety of the new parent from the pathological anxiety that characterizes GAD. In Cassie's case, however, it seems evident that her worry had become pathological.

Though "postpartum depression" has been well researched, comparatively little attention has been paid to anxiety disorders that arise during and soon after pregnancy. By the time Cassie met with a therapist, she had been suffering for several months, but she felt that since it was "just anxiety," she should just get over it. Had the severity of her anxiety been noticed earlier, she could have gotten into treatment before her anxiety symptoms worsened and she developed comorbid depression.

CASE 4: MAX—TEST ANXIETY

Max, a 17-year-old junior in high school, was approaching the date on which he was scheduled to take the SAT. Max felt pressured to do well on the exam because his parents couldn't afford the full cost of tuition and were relying on him to earn an academic scholarship. Attempting to be reassuring, Max's parents told him that they were completely sure that he would get the highest score in his class. Though well intentioned, these comments only made Max more distressed, as he contemplated the humiliation and shame he would feel when he inevitably disappointed them. Max tried to lower their expectations, but it didn't seem to be working.

Max had always gotten nervous before important exams, so he wasn't surprised to be feeling anxious. At the same time, Max's anxiety related to the SAT felt different than his typical pretest jitters. Usually, he only felt anxious a day or two before an examination, but this time, he began to notice symptoms four weeks before the test date. Max had also been caught off guard by the intensity of his physical symptoms. Due to his long history of test anxiety, Max had gotten accustomed to feeling some gastric distress before tests, but in the run-up to the SAT, just thinking about studying could trigger a wave of nausea. Similarly, he was used to feeling sharp spikes of anxiety in the moments before a test or quiz began, but in the past, his anxiety usually settled a few minutes after an exam started. During his preparation for the SAT, Max's anxiety followed a different pattern. When taking SAT practice tests, the spikes of anxiety happened whenever Max encountered a challenging question, and his anxiety took longer to subside. In fact, Max sometimes felt nervous even after the practice tests ended, which he had never experienced before.

The increase in Max's physiological distress was accompanied by worry thoughts. Max's worries became more and more common during the weeks leading up to the exam. At first, these thoughts happened only when he encountered something in his environment that was directly related to the exam, such as when his friends talked about where they were planning to apply to college. As the test neared, Max noticed that his worries got stuck in his mind for extended periods of time. He found the worries themselves to be unpleasant, but he was more upset by the way they clouded his thinking and wasted time that he needed to use for studying.

Though he was quite distressed by his anxiety, Max was reassured by the fact that his scores had generally been fine. However, after a catastrophic experience on a practice exam, Max's emotional distress began to interfere with his performance. During this practice test, Max became so overwhelmed by a combination of physiological symptoms and worry thoughts that he had to reread the same question many times. With a rising sense of panic, Max found himself unable to comprehend the question's meaning, let alone figure out the right answer. With great effort, Max forced himself to keep working, but he ran out of time with nearly half of the test items left blank.

After his disastrous performance on the practice test, Max repeatedly got stuck in self-perpetuating loops of anxiety: the loop started when Max would get a practice question wrong. He would then feel anxiety rising in his chest, notice stomach discomfort, and see that his hands were trembling. He would get distracted by self-defeating thoughts, telling himself that he would never get a scholarship. He would get lost in vividly imagined "daymares," which began with his mind going utterly blank on test day and ended with him being rejected by every college, or worse yet, his parents telling him that he needed to retake the test.

The test day arrived. Max barely slept the night before. He vomited once while getting ready and once on the way to school. Max felt anxious at the start of the test, but the feeling subsided soon after it began. He had a few moments of sharp panic when he couldn't immediately understand a question, but he settled down quickly. Max received his score in the mail and found that he did worse than he hoped, but much better than he feared.

Analysis

In modern society, high test scores can open the doors of opportunity, while low scores can seal them shut. Exams can impact where you are admitted to college, whether you are hired for a job, whether you earn professional certification, and they can determine your standing in the social hierarchy. Given their importance, it is not surprising that tests can be a source of stress.

As exemplified by Max, those who suffer from significant anxiety related to tests or other formal evaluations are labeled as having "test anxiety." Research suggests that test anxiety is a common problem, with one study estimating prevalence rates of 15 to 20 percent among college students and another study suggesting that 25 to 40 percent of students experience test anxiety. Researchers have found that test anxiety leads to impaired performance; highly test-anxious students score 12 percentile points below their low-anxiety peers.

Like other forms of anxiety, test anxiety is comprised of physiological, behavioral, and cognitive components. The physiological element refers to the physical symptoms of anxiety, which in Max's case, included gastric distress, elevated heart rate, and trembling hands. The behavioral aspect of test anxiety involves poor study skills, as well as inattentiveness and distraction during the test. The cognitive component is typified by thoughts that are unrelated to the test. Test-anxious people find it hard to concentrate on the task at hand because their attention is drawn toward negative cognitions (e.g., "I know I'm going to do poorly") and to thoughts about their physiological sensations (e.g., "Why can't I calm down?").

Test anxiety provides a real-world example of the Yerkes-Dodson law, which suggests that there is a relationship between arousal and performance that follows an "inverted U" shape. (See Question 17 titled "How does anxiety cause people to 'choke' under pressure?" for information on this topic.) At the lowest end of arousal, it's difficult to take a test when you're barely awake, and at the highest end, it's impossible to focus on a test when you're in the middle of a panic attack. The ideal amount of arousal lies between these extremes, enabling alertness without crossing the line to uncomfortable levels of anxiety. Treatments for test anxiety that are aimed at reducing physiological arousal have proven effective, as have those that focus on changing negative thoughts.

CASE 5: JON—POST-TRAUMATIC STRESS DISORDER

Jon, an 18-year-old from Boston, was traveling with his family to Israel. They stopped for pizza in Jerusalem, and Jon waited to order while his family sat outside. Jon's memory of the event was blurry from this point forward, but he vaguely recalled seeing a man enter the restaurant wearing a vest. Jon remembered being pushed to the ground by a soldier, the sensation of heat on his face, and the silence as he stood, bewildered, and exited the restaurant. His only vivid memory from that day was the terror he felt as he stepped past the unmoving body of a child, whom he momentarily mistook for his younger brother. Though Jon did not recall what happened next, he later learned that he had been found by paramedics, disoriented and incoherent, calling for his parents and siblings. Bleeding heavily from a wound to his leg, the paramedics had to drag him into the ambulance forcibly. His next memory was waking in a hospital bed with his family at his side.

Jon's parents explained that he had suffered a leg injury from shrapnel and burns across much of his body, but that he was expected to recover fully after a few surgeries and a couple of months of physical therapy. Jon seemed confused, on edge, and withdrawn for the first week in the hospital, but his parents felt that he was back to his normal self by the following week. Two months after the attack, Jon had regained his health sufficiently that he could return home to Boston.

Expecting that he would be upset, his parents informed Jon that he would have to take the semester off from school because he had already missed too much classwork. Jon reacted with an indifference that reminded his parents of a period in eighth grade when Jon was diagnosed with depression. His depression seemed to go away on its own soon after he was diagnosed, and his parents rarely thought about it in the years since. Jon's parents had been perplexed by how well he seemed to have responded in the immediate aftermath of the terrorist incident. Two months later, they separately noticed that he appeared to be more distant. Interactions with Jon had taken on a strange, detached quality; he sometimes trailed off mid-sentence, apparently contemplating something as he stared blankly into space.

Although he seemed to be lost in his own world, he was extremely aware of certain things. Even the slightest unexpected noise made him jump, and it could take him over an hour to regain his composure. When he left the house—which had become an uncommon occurrence—he kept a watchful eye on entrances and exits. If he saw anything that seemed "suspicious," which meant any person or object that bore even a superficial similarity to those present in the terrorist attack, he demanded that his friends or family leave immediately. Jon used to love pizza, but since the event, he had developed a growing aversion to what had once been his favorite food. First, Jon said that he didn't want to eat pizza anymore, then he didn't want pizza in the house, and a few months after the attack, he could not bear to see television commercials featuring pizza or to hear the word uttered by others. Finally, Jon had become preoccupied with knowing the schedules and whereabouts of his family members. When people did not return home at the time Jon expected, he would call and text them repeatedly until they answered. Jon, who had previously considered religion and spirituality central to his identity, abruptly stopped identifying as an Orthodox Jew. He still believed that God existed, but he now experienced God as a malignant force intent on making him suffer.

Jon would not admit this to anyone, but during moments when he appeared to be "spacing out," he was experiencing intense flashbacks that transported him back to the moment that he saw the dead child. His terror during the flashbacks gave way to extreme guilt and shame once he returned to the present moment. "Why did I deserve to live when so many other people died?" "Why didn't I rush toward the bomber and stop him?" Jon also suffered from a recurring nightmare in which he turned over the body of the child and saw his brother's face. These nightmares were so persistent and distressing that he began drinking coffee late at night to forestall sleep. When this stopped working, Jon turned to alcohol, since he had heard that alcohol disrupts dreaming. It was effective, but he soon found that he needed to drink more and more to keep the nightmares at bay.

Six months after the attack, Jon awoke once more in a hospital room with his parents by his side. This time, it was because he had been picked up by police for driving while intoxicated. The police report indicated that Jon sobbed uncontrollably and seemed unaware of his surroundings. Mirroring his experience six months earlier, Jon had been so distraught that he had to be forced into an ambulance. Jon, unable to recall his name or address, kept pleading with the paramedics to find his brother.

Analysis

Jon, as you may have surmised, suffers from post-traumatic stress disorder (PTSD). Jon's initial reaction to the event included cognitive, emotional, physical, and interpersonal symptoms. Such responses are relatively common in the immediate aftermath of a trauma, and their appearance does not necessarily indicate that someone will go on to develop PTSD. In fact, the overwhelming majority of those who experience a potentially traumatic event—and even those who develop acute stress disorder—never develop full-blown PTSD. Is there any explanation for why this happened to Jon?

It is impossible to determine why an individual develops PTSD and another does not, but some factors placed Jon at increased risk. For example, some features of the trauma itself made Jon more likely to develop PTSD. Terrorist attacks and other violent incidents are more apt to result in PTSD than nonviolent events, such as natural disasters. Jon was also at greater risk for PTSD due to his experience of "peritraumatic dissociation," which refers to disturbances in awareness, memory, and perception during and immediately after a traumatic event. In Jon's case, peritraumatic dissociation is evidenced by the disoriented state in which he was found by paramedics, as well as the gaps in his memory of the event. Furthermore, those who are most directly exposed to a traumatic event are more likely to develop PTSD, and Jon's exposure could not have been any more direct and intense. Lastly, even before the event, Jon was at greater risk of developing PTSD than other men of his age due to his history of depression.

Over a period of a few months after the event, Jon developed symptoms that were sufficient for a diagnosis of PTSD. His presentation included intrusive symptoms (e.g., distressing dreams and flashbacks), avoidant symptoms (including his growing aversion to pizza, attempts to delay sleep in an effort to avoid nightmares, and need to know the whereabouts of his family members), negative alterations in cognitions and moods associated with the event (inability to remember important aspects of the traumatic event, a distorted belief that he could have prevented the attack, and estrangement from others), and alterations in arousal and reactivity (exaggerated startle response, sleep disturbance, hypervigilance to signs of danger, and self-destructive behavior).

A variety of factors served to maintain Jon's PTSD. People are less likely to develop PTSD if they can continue to function normally in their work, academic, or social roles. Jon, being stuck in at a hospital in an unfamiliar country for two months, and having to take a leave of absence from college, was cut off from friendships and the normal rhythms of life, placing him at greater risk for developing both PTSD and depression. His PTSD was also maintained by the avoidance behaviors that proliferated after he returned home. These included the use of caffeine to avoid sleep, which is particularly problematic because sleep deprivation can cause heightened anxiety, and because caffeine does the same. Jon's use of alcohol as a method of regulating emotion also prolonged and exacerbated his symptoms, as it prevented him from learning that he could cope with reality and because alcohol use can provoke dissociation, lead to impaired cognition, and is associated with poorer emotional and social functioning.

Somewhat surprisingly, being religious placed Jon at greater risk for PTSD. A study in Israel, for example, found that religious Jews were three times more likely to develop PTSD following a trauma than those with secular beliefs. It is theorized that PTSD is more likely among religious victims of terror because of the appraisals they make about why the event happened. For the agnostic or atheist, a traumatic event, though terrible, is reducible to bad luck. No reevaluation of morality, truth, or one's place in the universe is needed. For the religious person who believes in God's omnipotence, a traumatic event may force some uncomfortable questions. "Maybe it was all my fault that this happened?" "Maybe God meant to punish me?" "Maybe God doesn't have the power to protect me?" "Maybe God is evil?" For Jon, the traumatic event led him to lose his sense of trust that God would protect him, making the world feel like a much more dangerous place. It also left him isolated from his community, which could have been a source of support.

Directory of Resources

INFORMATIONAL BOOKS

Adam, D. (2014). *The Man Who Couldn't Stop: OCD and the True Story of a Life Lost in Thought*. New York: Picador.

Rachman, S. J. (2013). *Anxiety* (3rd edition). New York: Psychology Press.

Sapolsky, R. M. (2004). *Why Zebras Don't Get Ulcers* (3rd edition). New York: Holt Paperbacks.

Sapolsky, R. M. (2017). *Behave: The Biology of Humans at Our Best and Worst*. New York: Penguin Press.

Stossel, S. (2013). *My Age of Anxiety: Fear, Hope, Dread, and the Search for Peace of Mind* (1st edition). New York: Alfred A. Knopf.

SELF-HELP BOOKS (BASED ON CBT)

Antony, M. M., Craske, M. G., & Barlow, D. H. (2006). *Mastering Your Fears and Phobias: Workbook* (2nd edition). Oxford; New York: Oxford University Press.

Antony, M. M., & Swinson R. P. (2008). *Shyness and Social Anxiety Workbook: Proven, Step-by-Step Techniques for Overcoming Your Fear* (2nd edition). Oakland, CA: New Harbinger.

Barlow, D. H., Ellard, K. K., Fairholme, C. P., Farchione, T. J., Boisseau, C. L., May, J. T. E., & Allen, L. B. (2010). *Unified Protocol for Transdiagnostic*

Treatment of Emotional Disorders: Workbook (Workbook edition). New York: Oxford University Press.

Burns, D. D. (2011). *Feeling Good: The New Mood Therapy* (2nd edition). New York: Harper Collins.

Foa, E. B., & Wilson, R. (2001). *Stop Obsessing!: How to Overcome Your Obsessions and Compulsions* (1st edition). New York: Bantam.

ORGANIZATIONS

American Academy of Child and Adolescent Psychiatry—www.aacap.org

The American Psychiatric Association—www.psychiatry.org

The American Psychological Association—www.apa.org

Anxiety and Depression Association of America—www.adaa.org

International OCD Foundation—www.ocfoundation.org

International Society for Traumatic Stress Studies—www.istss.org

National Alliance on Mental Illness—www.nami.org

National Center for Post-Traumatic Stress Disorders—www.ncptsd.va.gov

National Institute of Mental Health—www.nimh.nih.gov

uptodate.com (provides physicians and therapists with evidence-based treatment recommendations based on current research)

FINDING PROFESSIONAL HELP

Anxiety and Depression Association of America—www.treatment.adaa.org

Association for Behavioral and Cognitive Therapies—www.abctcentral .org/xFAT/

National Alliance on Mental Illness (NAMI)—https://www.nami.org/ Find-Support/NAMI-HelpLine or call 1-800-950-NAMI (6264)

National Institute of Mental Health—www.nimh.nih.gov/findhelp

Psychology Today—www.psychologytoday.com/

Substance Abuse and Mental Health Services Administration (SAMHSA)—www.findtreatment.samhsa.gov/

HOTLINES (UNITED STATES ONLY)

National Alliance on Mental Illness (NAMI) Crisis Text Line—Text "NAMI" to 741-741

National Domestic Violence Hotline—Call 800-799-SAFE (7233)

National Hopeline Network—800-784-2433

National Sexual Assault Hotline—Call 800-656-HOPE (4673)

National Suicide Prevention Lifeline—800-273-TALK (273-8255)

NIMH's National Anxiety Hotline—888-ANXIETY (826-9438)

Panic Disorder Information Hotline—800-64-PANIC (647-2642)

Substance Abuse and Mental Health Services Administration (SAMHSA) National Helpline: 1-800-662-HELP (4357)

Teen Line: 1-310-855-HOPE (4673) or 1-800-TLC-TEEN (1-800-852-8336); can also be reached by texting "TEEN" to 839863.

If you are experiencing a crisis, call 9-1-1 or go to your nearest emergency room.

Glossary

Acute stress disorder: a diagnosis that describes certain cognitive, emotional, and behavioral symptoms that develop in the aftermath of one or more traumatic experiences. Acute stress disorder may be diagnosed for the first 30 days after a traumatic event, after which the affected individual's diagnosis would shift to post-traumatic stress disorder.

Adrenaline: also known as epinephrine, adrenaline is a hormone and neurotransmitter that is released as part of the fight–flight–freeze response to perceived danger.

Agoraphobia: an anxiety disorder characterized by a fear of situations in which escape could be difficult, or in which help would not be available if it was needed.

Amygdala: a brain region that is involved in generating the fear response.

Antidepressant: drugs that are typically, though not exclusively, used in the treatment of depression and anxiety.

Anxiety: the anticipation of future threat that is accompanied by distress, physical tension, and/or worry.

Anxiety disorder: a mental illness characterized by maladaptive and disproportionately high levels of fear and/or anxiety.

Anxiety hierarchy: a rank-ordered list of anxiety-provoking situations that is typically used in cognitive-behavioral therapy.

Arousal: the physiological state of alertness and responsiveness to stimuli.

Associative learning: the process through which an organism learns that two stimuli are associated with one another.

Attachment theory: a psychological theory based on the idea that one's early relationships with caregivers have an impact on their subsequent development.

Automatic thoughts: thoughts that arise automatically and without conscious evaluation in response to a stimulus. In those who have high levels of anxiety, these thoughts tend to be biased toward critical self-judgments or toward the overprediction of negative outcomes.

Autonomic nervous system: the part of the peripheral nervous system that regulates unconscious bodily functions. The autonomic nervous system is comprised of the sympathetic nervous system, which is instrumental in the fight–flight–freeze response, and the parasympathetic nervous system, which controls the functioning of the body while at rest and returns the body to a calm state.

Avoidance behavior: an action that is meant to help an individual avoid a situation, activity, object, or thought that may generate distress in the future.

Behavioral inhibition: a pattern of behaviors that is associated with shyness and social anxiety.

Behavioral therapy: a form of psychotherapy, drawn from the fields of behaviorism and learning theory, that aims to change maladaptive behaviors using methods that include reinforcement and exposure.

Benzodiazepines: a class of drugs frequently prescribed for anxiety disorders, which exerts its effect by increasing the activity of the inhibitory neurotransmitter, GABA.

Beta-blocker: a class of drugs that is typically prescribed to treat cardiac arrhythmia but which is also used as off-label treatment for the physiological symptoms of anxiety.

Cingulotomy: sometimes used as a treatment for severe depression or obsessive-compulsive disorder, cingulotomy is a form of brain surgery that involves destroying the anterior cingulate gyrus.

Classical conditioning: also known as Pavlovian conditioning, this refers to a learning procedure in which a neutral stimulus is repeatedly paired with an unconditioned stimulus (i.e., a stimulus that naturally evokes a response), such that the previously neutral stimulus comes to elicit the same response.

Cognitive-behavioral therapy: a form of psychotherapy that combines cognitive and behavioral approaches and seeks to improve the patient's functioning by reducing maladaptive behaviors, increasing adaptive behaviors, and modifying thoughts that are maintaining the illness.

Cognitive distortion: common errors in thinking, which, in people with problematic anxiety, lead to overly negative perceptions of the present, to the overprediction of future risk, and to general negative mood.

Cognitive restructuring: commonly associated with CBT, cognitive restructuring involves teaching the client to identify maladaptive and/or irrational thoughts, challenge them with evidence or reason, and replace them with more accurate and/or adaptive thoughts.

Cognitive therapy: a form of psychotherapy based on the idea that thoughts determine behavior and emotion, and that correcting inaccurate or maladaptive thoughts will lead to therapeutic change.

Comorbidity: the presence of multiple disorders in the same individual.

Compulsion: repetitive mental rituals or behaviors, which in those with OCD, the individual feels he or she must perform in reaction to an obsession.

Culture: rules, beliefs, concepts, knowledge, and practices that are shared among a group of people and across generations.

Deep brain stimulation: a treatment for severe depression and OCD in which a device is surgically implanted in the patient. This device transmits electrical signals that alter the functioning of a brain region associated with addictive behaviors.

Defense mechanisms: emanating from Freud, defense mechanisms are unconscious strategies that an individual uses to cope with reality.

Depression: a mental illness characterized by sad mood (referred to in the *DSM* as "major depressive disorder").

Diagnosis: the identified illness.

Diagnostic and Statistical Manual of Mental Disorders (DSM): Currently in its fifth revision after an update in 2013, the *DSM* provides a list of mental disorders and their diagnostic criteria, and is used by researchers and clinicians to classify mental disorders.

Dissociation: a disruption in the functioning of memory, identity, or consciousness, which may involve an alteration in one's experience of oneself (depersonalization) and/or one's surroundings (derealization).

Emetophobia: a specific phobia of vomiting.

Epidemiology: the study of the distribution and sources of illness in a population.

Escape behavior: an action that is meant to help an individual escape a situation, activity, object, or thought that is generating distress in the present.

Etiology: the cause or causes of a disease.

Exposure therapy: a therapeutic technique that is typically used in CBT, in which an individual is exposed to a feared situation or object so that he or she learns to evaluate risk more accurately and to manage distress in a more effective manner.

Fear: an emotional response to the perception of an imminent threat.

Fight, fight, or freeze response (often shortened to "fight or flight response"): a physiological response to a perceived threat that prepares an organism to fight, flee, or stay still.

Flashback: a dissociative state seen in those with PTSD in which an individual feels as though he or she is reexperiencing aspects of a traumatic event in the present moment.

Humoral theory (four humors): belief, originating in Classical Greece, that illness and temperament were caused by an excess or deficiency in the four bodily fluids, or humors.

Gamma-aminobutyric acid (GABA): the main inhibitory neurotransmitter in the central nervous system, the functioning of which is modified by the benzodiazepine class of medications.

Gene: a gene is a segment of DNA that represents the basic unit of heredity.

Generalized anxiety disorder: anxiety disorder characterized by persistent anxiety and worries across multiple domains, as well as physiological symptoms of anxiety.

Heritability: an estimate of the extent to which variation in a particular trait in a population is attributable to genetic differences between individuals in that population.

Hypervigilance: a state of heightened sensitivity to threat, characterized by high arousal, exaggerated behavioral responses to stimuli, and constant scanning for potential threats.

Maladaptive: a term that refers to thoughts, emotions, or behaviors that cause suffering or dysfunction.

Median: in a set of numbers, the median is the number that falls in the middle of the distribution.

Meta-analysis: a research technique that analyzes many scientific studies together to reach a unified conclusion.

Mood: a sustained emotional state that, in comparison to emotion, is less likely to be provoked by a particular stimulus.

Negative reinforcement: a behavioral technique in which a behavior is increased or strengthened by the removal of an aversive stimulus.

Neuron: the most common type of cell in the brain.

Neurotransmitter: a chemical messenger that allows neurons to communicate electrical impulses to neighboring cells.

Obsession: one of the core symptoms of OCD, obsessions are recurrent and unwanted thoughts, urges, or images that typically lead to distress.

Obsessive-compulsive disorder: disorder characterized by repetitive, distressing, and unwanted thoughts and ritualized mental or behavioral responses aimed at reducing distress elicited by the thoughts.

Panic attack: an abrupt surge of fear or physiological discomfort that reaches its peak within a few minutes and which is accompanied by certain cognitive and/or physiological symptoms.

Panic disorder: diagnosis assigned to those who experience recurrent unexpected panic attacks. People with panic disorder experience persistent worry about future panic attacks and/or they make maladaptive changes to their behavior to reduce the risk of having additional panic attacks.

Positive reinforcement: a behavioral technique in which a behavior is increased or strengthened by the application of a reinforcer. This is contrasted with a "punisher," which reduces or weakens a behavior.

Post-traumatic stress disorder: a diagnosis that is assigned when an individual develops certain physiological, emotional, cognitive, and behavioral symptoms in response to one or more traumatic events.

Prevalence: the proportion of a population that currently has, or who has had, an illness over a given span of time.

Psychiatrist: a medical doctor who has received specialized training in the treatment of mental illness. Psychiatrists generally prescribe medication, but they may also offer psychotherapy. Medications are also often prescribed by psychiatric nurse practitioners, who have degrees in nursing.

Psychoanalysis: a type of psychotherapy developed by Sigmund Freud that sees mental illness as the result of internal, unconscious conflict. Psychoanalysis aims to bring unconscious conflict into conscious awareness.

Psychologist: psychologists who provide psychotherapy are called clinical psychologists, school psychologists, or counseling psychologists. In most states, clinical psychologists must have a doctoral degree and must be licensed to practice.

Psychotherapy: the treatment of mental disorders using psychological methods as opposed to medical interventions.

Risk factor: variables that are associated with an increased likelihood of a given illness.

Safety behavior: a form of avoidance behavior in which an individual relies on an object or person to reduce his or her anxiety or to reduce the likelihood of a feared event.

Selective mutism: anxiety disorder typically diagnosed in children, which is assigned to those who are capable of speech in some situations, but who consistently fail to speak in other social situation in which there is an expectation of speech.

Separation anxiety disorder: anxiety disorder, generally diagnosed in children, involving disproportionate anxiety or fear about separation from attachment figures and/or home.

Social anxiety disorder: anxiety disorder diagnosed in those who experience disproportionate anxiety, fear, or avoidance of social interactions in which they may be evaluated by others.

Specific phobia: anxiety disorder characterized by disproportionate fear, anxiety, or avoidance of certain situations or objects.

State anxiety: unpleasant arousal in response to a particular stimulus.

Symptom: a manifestation of an illness that is reported by the patient (whereas a "sign" is a manifestation of an illness that is observed by the examiner).

Temperament: biologically based behavioral patterns and character traits that are stable across multiple contexts.

Trait anxiety: a stable tendency to respond with state anxiety in response to many situations.

Triune brain: developed in the 1960s by Paul McLean, the triune brain is a model of the brain's evolution and functional organization that divides the brain into three layers.

Worry: the cognitive component of anxiety, worries typically involve emotionally laden thoughts about an anticipated threat and pessimistic predictions about one's ability to cope with the threat.

Yerkes-Dodson law: the psychological principle that describes the relationship between arousal and task performance.

Bibliography

Ainsworth, M. D. S., Blehar, M. C., Waters, E., & Wall, S. (1978). *Patterns of Attachment: A Psychological Study of the Strange Situation*. Hillsdale, NJ: Erlbaum.

Barlow, D. H. (2002). *Anxiety and Its Disorders: The Nature and Treatment of Anxiety and Panic* (2nd edition). New York: Guilford Press.

Barnes, P. M., Bloom, B., & Nahin, R. L. (2008). "Complementary and Alternative Medicine Use among Adults and Children: United States, 2007." *National Health Statistics Reports*, 10(12), 1–23.

Barnes, P. M., Powell-Griner, E., McFann, K., & Nahin, R. L. (2004). "Complementary and Alternative Medicine Use among Adults: United States, 2002." *Advance Data*, (343), 1–19.

Barrera, T. L., Wilson, K. P., & Norton, P. J. (2010). "The Experience of Panic Symptoms across Racial Groups in a Student Sample." *Journal of Anxiety Disorders*, 24(8), 873–878.

Bateson, M., Brilot, B., & Nettle, D. (2011). "Anxiety: An Evolutionary Approach." *Canadian Journal of Psychiatry*, 56(12), 707–715.

Beesdo, K., Hoyer, J., Jacobi, F., Low, N. C. P., Höfler, M., & Wittchen, H.-U. (2009). "Association between Generalized Anxiety Levels and Pain in a Community Sample: Evidence for Diagnostic Specificity." *Journal of Anxiety Disorders*, 23(5), 684–693. https://doi.org/10.1016/j.janxdis.2009.02.007.

Berrios, G. (1999). "Anxiety Disorders: A Conceptual History." *Journal of Affective Disorders*, 56(2), 83–94.

Bruce, S. E., Yonkers, K. A., Otto, M. W., Eisen, J. L., Weisberg, R. B., Pagano, M., . . ., Keller, M. B. (2005). "Influence of Psychiatric Comorbidity on Recovery and Recurrence in Generalized Anxiety Disorder, Social Phobia, and Panic Disorder: A 12-Year Prospective Study." *American Journal of Psychiatry*, 162(6), 1179–1187.

Bystritsky, A., Hovav, S., Sherbourne, C., Stein, M. B., Rose, R. D., Campbell-Sills, L., . . ., Roy-Byrne, P. P. (2012). "Use of Complementary and Alternative Medicine in a Large Sample of Anxiety Patients." *Psychosomatics*, 53(3), 266–272.

Bystritsky, A., Stein, M., & Hermann, R. (2016). "Complementary and Alternative Treatments for Anxiety Symptoms and Disorders: Physical, Cognitive, and Spiritual Interventions." In R. Hermann (Ed.), *UpToDate*. Retrieved July 10, 2016, from http://www.upto date.com/contents/complementary-and-alternative-treatments-for-anxiety-symptoms-and-disorders-physical-cognitive-and-spiritual-interventions.

Cannon, W. (1927). "The James-Lange Theory of Emotions: A Critical Examination and an Alternative Theory." *American Journal of Psychology*, 39(1/4), 106–124.

Cassady, J. C. (2010). "Test Anxiety: Contemporary Theories and Implications for Learning." In J. C. Cassady (Ed.), *Anxiety in Schools: The Causes, Consequences, and Solutions for Academic Anxieties* (pp. 7–26). New York: Peter Lang.

Cassady, J. C., & Johnson, R. E. (2002). "Cognitive Test Anxiety and Academic Performance." *Contemporary Educational Psychology*, 27, 270–295.

Chaplin, T. M., Hong, K., Bergquist, K., & Sinha, R. (2008). "Gender Differences in Response to Emotional Stress: An Assessment across Subjective, Behavioral, and Physiological Domains and Relations to Alcohol Craving." *Alcoholism, Clinical and Experimental Research*, 32(7), 1242–1250.

Clark, G. I., & Rock, A. J. (2016). "Processes Contributing to the Maintenance of Flying Phobia: A Narrative Review." *Frontiers in Psychology*, 7, 764.

Clark, L. A., & Watson, D. (1991). "Tripartite Model of Anxiety and Depression: Psychometric Evidence and Taxonomic Implications." *Journal of Abnormal Psychology*, 100(3), 316–336.

Coutinho, F.C., Dias, G.P., Nascimento Bevilaqua, M.C. do, Gardino, P.F., Rangé, B.P., & Nardi, A.E. (2010). "Current Concept of Anxiety: Implications from Darwin to the DSM-V for the Diagnosis of Generalized Anxiety Disorder." *Expert Review of Neurotherapeutics*, 10(8), 1307–1320.

Craske, M.G., Rauch, S.L., Ursano, R., Prenoveau, J., Pine, D.S., & Zinbarg, R.E. (2009). "What Is an Anxiety Disorder?" *Depression and Anxiety*, 26(12), 1066–1085.

Craske, M.G., & Stein, M.B. (2016). "Anxiety." *Lancet*, 388(10063), 3048–3059.

Craske, M.G., Stein, M.B., Eley, T.C., Milad, M.R., Holmes, A., Rapee, R.M., & Wittchen, H.U. (2017). "Anxiety Disorders." *Nature Reviews Disease Primers*, 3, 17024.

Crocq, M.-A. (2015). "A History of Anxiety: From Hippocrates to DSM." *Dialogues in Clinical Neuroscience*, 17(3), 319–325.

Darwin, C.R. (1872). *The Expression of the Emotions in Man and Animals* (1st edition). London: John Murray.

Dekel, S., Stuebe, C., & Dishy, G. (2017). "Childbirth Induced Posttraumatic Stress Syndrome: A Systematic Review of Prevalence and Risk Factors." *Frontiers in Psychology*, 8, 560.

Doctor, R.M., Kahn, A.P., & Adamec, C.A. (2008). *The Encyclopedia of Phobias, Fears, and Anxieties* (3rd edition). New York: Facts on File.

Ergene, T. (2003). "Effective Interventions on Test Anxiety Reduction: A Meta-Analysis." *School Psychology International*, 24(3), 313–328.

Fernández de la Cruz, L., Rydell, M., Runeson, B., D'Onofrio, B.M., Brander, G., Rück, C., & Mataix-Cols, D. (2017). "Suicide in Obsessive–Compulsive Disorder: A Population-Based Study of 36 788 Swedish Patients." *Molecular Psychiatry*, 22(11), 1626–1632.

Fisak, B., & Grills-Taquechel, A.E. (2007). "Parental Modeling, Reinforcement, and Information Transfer: Risk Factors in the Development of Child Anxiety?" *Clinical Child and Family Psychology Review*, 10(3), 213–231.

Fleet, R.P., Dupuis, G., Marchand, A., Burelle, D., & Beitman, B.D. (1997). "Detecting Panic Disorder in Emergency Department Chest Pain Patients: A Validated Model to Improve Recognition." *Annals of Behavioral Medicine*, 19(2), 124–131.

Frances, A. (2014). *Saving Normal: An Insider's Revolt against Out-of-Control Psychiatric Diagnosis, DSM-5, Big Pharma, and the Medicalization of Ordinary Life* (1st reprint edition). New York: William Morrow Paperbacks.

Haidich, A. B. (2010). "Meta-Analysis in Medical Research." *Hippokratia*, 14(Suppl. 1), 29–37.

Hasler, B., & Germain, A. (2009). "Correlates and Treatments of Nightmares in Adults." *Sleep Medicine Clinics*, 4(4), 507–517.

Helwick, C. (2011). "Anxiety 'Density' in Families Predicts Disorders in Children." Retrieved October 28, 2017, from https://www.medscape.com/viewarticle/739731.

Herek, G. M. (2004). "Beyond 'Homophobia': Thinking about Sexual Prejudice and Stigma in the Twenty-First Century." *Sexuality Research & Social Policy*, 1(2), 6–24.

Hettema, J. M., Neale, M. C., & Kendler, K. S. (2001). "A Review and Meta-Analysis of the Genetic Epidemiology of Anxiety Disorders." *American Journal of Psychiatry*, 158(10), 1568–1578.

Hettema, J. M., Prescott, C. A., Myers, J. M., Neale, M. C., & Kendler, K. S. (2005). "The Structure of Genetic and Environmental Risk Factors for Anxiety Disorders in Men and Women." *Archives of General Psychiatry*, 62(2), 182–189.

Higginson, T. W. (1865). *The Works of Epictetus. Consisting of His Discourses, in Four Books, The Enchiridion, and Fragments.* Boston, MA: Little, Brown, and Co.

Hill, K. T., & Wigfield, A. (1984). "Test Anxiety: A Major Educational Problem and What Can Be Done about It." *Elementary School Journal*, 85(1), 105–126.

Hobfoll, S. E., Canetti-Nisim, D., Johnson, R. J., Palmieri, P. A., Varley, J. D., & Galea, S. (2008). "The Association of Exposure, Risk, and Resiliency Factors with PTSD among Jews and Arabs Exposed to Repeated Acts of Terrorism in Israel." *Journal of Traumatic Stress*, 21(1), 9–21.

Horwitz, A. V. (2013). *Anxiety: A Short History.* Baltimore, MD: Johns Hopkins University Press.

Hranov, L. G. (2007). "Comorbid Anxiety and Depression: Illumination of a Controversy." *International Journal of Psychiatry in Clinical Practice*, 11(3), 171–189.

Hudson, J. L. (2012). "Parent-Child Relationships in Early Childhood and Development of Anxiety & Depression." Parenting Skills. Retrieved from http://www.child-encyclopedia.com/sites/default/files/dossiers-complets/en/parenting-skills.pdf#page=47.

Jorm, A. F., Christensen, H., Griffiths, K. M., Parslow, R. A., Rodgers, B., & Blewitt, K. A. (2004). "Effectiveness of Complementary and Self-Help Treatments for Anxiety Disorders." *Medical Journal of Australia*, 181(7), 29.

Kahneman, D. (2011). *Thinking, Fast and Slow* (1st edition.). New York: Farrar, Straus and Giroux.

Kawachi, I., Sparrow, D., Vokonas, P. S., & Weiss, S. T. (1994). "Symptoms of Anxiety and Risk of Coronary Heart Disease. The Normative Aging Study." *Circulation*, 90(5), 2225–2229.

Kazantzis, N., & Lampropoulos, G. K. (2002). "Reflecting on Homework in Psychotherapy: What Can We Conclude from Research and Experience?" *Journal of Clinical Psychology*, 58(5):577–585.

Kendler, K. S., Myers, J., Prescott, C. A., & Neale, M. C. (2001). "The Genetic Epidemiology of Irrational Fears and Phobias in Men." *Archives of General Psychiatry*, 58:257–265.

Kendler, K. S., Neale, M. C., Kessler, R. C., Heath, A. C., & Eaves, L. J. (1992). "Childhood Parental Loss and Adult Psychopathology in Women: A Twin Study Perspective." *Archives of General Psychiatry*, 49(2), 109–116.

Kessler, R. C., Angermeyer, M., Anthony, J. C., De Graaf, R., Demyttenaere, K., Gasquet, I., & Ustun, T. B. (2007). "Lifetime Prevalence and Age-of-Onset Distributions of Mental Disorders in the World Health Organization's World Mental Health Survey Initiative." *World Psychiatry*, 6(3), 168–176.

Kessler, R. C., Rose, S., Koenen, K. C., Karam, E. G., Stang, P. E., Stein, D. J., & Carmen Viana, M. (2014). "How Well Can Post-Traumatic Stress Disorder Be Predicted from Pre-Trauma Risk Factors? An Exploratory Study in the WHO World Mental Health Surveys." *World Psychiatry*, 13(3), 265–274.

Kessler, R. C., Ruscio, A. M., Shear, K., & Wittchen, H. U. (2010). "Epidemiology of Anxiety Disorders." *Current Topics in Behavioral Neurosciences*, 2, 21–35.

Kessler, R. C., Sonnega, A., Bromet, E., Hughes, M., & Nelson, C. B. (1995). "Posttraumatic Stress Disorder in the National Comorbidity Survey." *Archives of General Psychiatry*, 52(12), 1048–1060.

Kessler, R. C., Soukup, J., Davis, R. B., Foster, D. F., Wilkey, S. A., Van Rompay, M. I., & Eisenberg, D. M. (2001). "The Use of Complementary and Alternative Therapies to Treat Anxiety and Depression in the United States." *American Journal of Psychiatry*, 158(2), 289–294.

Koenen, K. C., Amstadter, A. B., Ruggiero, K. J., Acierno, R., Galea, S., Kilpatrick, D. G., & Gelernter, J. (2009). "RGS2 and Generalized Anxiety Disorder in an Epidemiologic Sample of Hurricane-Exposed Adults." *Depression and Anxiety*, 26(4), 309–315.

Lahat, A., Hong, M., & Fox, N. A. (2011). "Behavioural Inhibition: Is It a Risk Factor for Anxiety?" *International Review of Psychiatry*, 23(3), 248–257.

Laurin, J. C., Joussemet, M., Tremblay, R. E., & Boivin, M. (2015). "Early Forms of Controlling Parenting and the Development of Childhood Anxiety." *Journal of Child and Family Studies*, 24(11), 3279–3292.

LeBeau, R. T., Glenn, D., Liao, B., Wittchen, H.-U., Beesdo-Baum, K., Ollendick, T., & Craske, M. G. (2010). "Specific Phobia: A Review of DSM-IV Specific Phobia and Preliminary Recommendations for DSM-V." *Depression and Anxiety*, 27(2), 148–167.

LeDoux, J. E. (1998). *The Emotional Brain: The Mysterious Underpinnings of Emotional Life* (1st Touchstone edition). New York: Simon & Schuster.

LeDoux, J. E. (2015). *Anxious: Using the Brain to Understand and Treat Fear and Anxiety*. New York: Viking Press.

Lee, Y.-L., Wu, Y., Tsang, H. W. H., Leung, A. Y., & Cheung, W. M. (2011). "A Systematic Review on the Anxiolytic Effects of Aromatherapy in People with Anxiety Symptoms." *Journal of Alternative and Complementary Medicine*, 17(2), 101–108.

Lydiard, R. B., Laraia, M. T., Howell, E. F., & Ballenger, J. C. (1986). "Can Panic Disorder Present as Irritable Bowel Syndrome?" *Journal of Clinical Psychiatry*, 47(9), 470–473.

McDonald, A. (2001). "The Prevalence and Effects of Test Anxiety in Children." *Educational Psychology*, 21(1), 89–101.

McHenry, J., Carrier, N., Hull, E., & Kabbaj, M. (2014). "Sex Differences in Anxiety and Depression: Role of Testosterone." *Frontiers in Neuroendocrinology*, 35(1), 42–57.

McLean, C. P., & Anderson, E. R. (2009). "Brave Men and Timid Women? A Review of the Gender Differences in Fear and Anxiety." *Clinical Psychology Review*, 29(6), 496–505.

McLean, C. P., Asnaani, A., Litz, B. T., & Hofmann, S. G. (2011). "Gender Differences in Anxiety Disorders: Prevalence, Course of Illness, Comorbidity and Burden of Illness." *Journal of Psychiatric Research*, 45(8), 1027–1035.

Merikangas, K. R., & Pine, D. (2002). "Genetic and Other Vulnerability Factors for Anxiety and Stress Disorders." In K. L. Davis, D. Charney, J. T. Coyle, & C. Nemeroff (Eds.), *Neuropsychopharmacology: The Fifth Generation of Progress* (pp. 867–882). Philadelphia, PA: Lippincott, Williams, & Wilkins.

Meuret, A. E., Rosenfield, D., Wilhelm, F. H., Zhou, E., Conrad, A., Ritz, T., & Roth, W. T. (2011). "Do Unexpected Panic Attacks Occur Spontaneously?" *Biological Psychiatry*, 70(10), 985–991.

Mineka, S., Watson, D., & Clark, L. A. (1998). "Comorbidity of Anxiety and Unipolar Mood Disorders." *Annual Review of Psychology*, 49, 377–412.

Mujica-Parodi, L. R., Strey, H. H., Frederick, B., Savoy, R., Cox, D., Botanov, Y., . . ., Weber, J. (2009). "Chemosensory Cues to Conspecific Emotional Stress Activate Amygdala in Humans." *PLoS ONE*, 4(7), e6415.

Muris, P., Ollendick, T. H., Roelofs, J., & Austin, K. (2014). "The Short Form of the Fear Survey Schedule for Children-Revised (FSSC-R-SF): An Efficient, Reliable, and Valid Scale for Measuring Fear in Children and Adolescents." *Journal of Anxiety Disorders*, 28(8), 957–965.

National Institute for Health and Care Excellence. (2014). "Anxiety Disorders." NICE Guideline (QS53).

NIMH. (n. d.). "What Is Prevalence?" Retrieved November 3, 2017, from https://www.nimh.nih.gov/health/statistics/prevalence/index.shtml.

Norton, G. R., Cox, B. J., & Malan, J. (1992). "Nonclinical Panickers: A Critical Review." *Clinical Psychology Review*, 12(2), 121–139.

O'Connor, T. G., Heron, J., Golding, J., Beveridge, M., & Glover, V. (2002). "Maternal Antenatal Anxiety and Children's Behavioural/Emotional Problems at 4 Years. Report from the Avon Longitudinal Study of Parents and Children." *British Journal of Psychiatry*, 180, 502–508.

Öhman, A., & Mineka, S. (2001). "Fear, Phobias and Preparedness: Toward an Evolved Module of Fear and Fear Learning." *Psychological Review*, 108(3), 483–522.

Otto, M. W., Tuby, K. S., Gould, R. A., McLean, R. Y., & Pollack, M. H. (2001). "An Effect-Size Analysis of the Relative Efficacy and Tolerability of Serotonin Selective Reuptake Inhibitors for Panic Disorder." *American Journal of Psychiatry*, 158(12), 1989–1992.

Pepper, J., Hariz, M., & Zrinzo, L. (2015). "Deep Brain Stimulation versus Anterior Capsulotomy for Obsessive-Compulsive Disorder: A Review of the Literature." *Journal of Neurosurgery*, 122(5), 1028–1037.

Preter, M., & Klein, D. F. (2008). "Panic, Suffocation False Alarms, Separation Anxiety and Endogenous Opioids." *Progress in Neuro-Psychopharmacology & Biological Psychiatry*, 32(3), 603–612.

Pummel, M. B. (2008). "Selective Mutism." Retrieved from http://ed-psych.utah.edu/school-psych/_documents/grants/specific-disabilities/selective-mutism-monograph.pdf.

Rand, D. G., & Epstein, Z. G. (2014). "Risking Your Life without a Second Thought: Intuitive Decision-Making and Extreme Altruism." *PLoS ONE*, 9(10), e109687.

Rodebaugh, T. L., Lim, M. H., Fernandez, K. C., Langer, J. K., Weisman, J. S., Tonge, N., . . ., Shumaker, E. A. (2014). "Self and Friend's Differing Views of Social Anxiety Disorder's Effects on Friendships." *Journal of Abnormal Psychology*, 123(4), 715–724.

Ross, L. E., & McLean, L. M. (2006). "Anxiety Disorders during Pregnancy and the Postpartum Period: A Systematic Review." *Journal of Clinical Psychiatry*, 67(8), 1285–1298.

Roy-Byrne, P. P., Craske, M. G., & Stein, M. B. (2006). "Panic Disorder." *Lancet*, 368(9540), 1023–1032.

Roy-Byrne, P. P., Stang, P., Wittchen, H. U., Ustun, B., Walters, E. E., & Kessler, R. C. (2000). "Lifetime Panic-Depression Comorbidity in the National Comorbidity Survey. Association with Symptoms, Impairment, Course and Help-Seeking." *British Journal of Psychiatry*, 176, 229–235.

Saleem, S., & Mahmood, Z. (2009). "OCD in a Cultural Context: A Phenomenological Approach." *Pakistan Journal of Psychological Research*, 24(1), 27–42.

Sayyah, M., Olapour, A., Saeedabad, Y. Shahhosseini, Yazdan Parast, R., & Malayeri, A. (2012). "Evaluation of Oral Zinc Sulfate Effect on Obsessive-Compulsive Disorder: A Randomized Placebo-Controlled Clinical Trial." *Nutrition*, 28(9), 892–895.

Schachter, S., & Singer, J. E. (1962). "Cognitive, Social, and Physiological Determinants of Emotional State." *Psychological Review*, 69(5), 375–399.

Scherrer, J. F., True, W. R., Xian, H., Lyons, M. J., Eisen, S. A., Goldberg, J., . . ., Tsuang, M. T. (2000). "Evidence for Genetic Influences Common and Specific to Symptoms of Generalized Anxiety and Panic." *Journal of Affective Disorders*, 57, 25–35.

Sharp, W. G., Sherman, C., & Gross, A. M. (2007). "Selective Mutism and Anxiety: A Review of the Current Conceptualization of the Disorder." *Journal of Anxiety Disorders*, 21(4), 568–579.

Shea, S. E., Gordon, K., Hawkins, A., Kawchuk, J., & Smith, D. (2000). "Pathology in the Hundred Acre Wood: A Neurodevelopmental Perspective on A.A. Milne." *Canadian Medical Association Journal*, 163(12), 1557–1559.

Sheth, S. A., Neal, J., Tangherlini, F., Mian, M. K., Gentil, A., Cosgrove, G. R., & Dougherty, D. D. (2013). "Limbic System Surgery for Treatment-Refractory Obsessive-Compulsive Disorder: A Prospective Long-Term Follow-Up of 64 Patients." *Journal of Neurosurgery*, 118(3), 491–497.

Shumyatsky, G. P., Malleret, G., Shin, R.-M., Takizawa, S., Tully, K., Tsvetkov, E., . . ., Bolshakov, V. Y. (2005). "stathmin, a Gene Enriched in the Amygdala, Controls Both Learned and Innate Fear." *Cell*, 123(4), 697–709.

Silverman, J. J., Singh, N. N., Carmanico, S. J., Lindstrom, K. A., Best, A. M., & Clearfield, S. (1999). "Psychological Distress and Symptoms of Posttraumatic Stress Disorder in Jewish Adolescents

Following a Brief Exposure to Concentration Camps." *Journal of Child and Family Studies*, 8(1), 71–89.

Smid, G. E., Mooren, T. T. M., van der Mast, R. C., Gersons, B. P. R., & Kleber, R. J. (2009). "Delayed Posttraumatic Stress Disorder: Systematic Review, Meta-Analysis, and Meta-Regression Analysis of Prospective Studies." *Journal of Clinical Psychiatry*, 70(11), 1572–1582.

Smoller, J. W. (2016). "The Genetics of Stress-Related Disorders: PTSD, Depression, and Anxiety Disorders." *Neuropsychopharmacology*, 41(1), 297–319.

Smoller, J. W., Block, S. R., & Young, M. M. (2009). "Genetics of Anxiety Disorders: The Complex Road from DSM to DNA." *Depression and Anxiety*, 26(11), 965–975.

Spence, S. H., Rapee, R., McDonald, C., & Ingram, M. (2001). "The Structure of Anxiety Symptoms among Preschoolers." *Behaviour Research and Therapy*, 39(11), 1293–1316.

Sroufe, L. A. (2005). "Attachment and Development: A Prospective, Longitudinal Study from Birth to Adulthood." *Attachment & Human Development*, 7(4), 349–367.

Steel, Z., Marnane, C., Iranpour, C., Chey, T., Jackson, J. W., Patel, V., & Silove, D. (2014). "The Global Prevalence of Common Mental Disorders: A Systematic Review and Meta-Analysis 1980–2013." *International Journal of Epidemiology*, 43(2), 476–493.

Stefanucci, J. K., Proffitt, D. R., Clore, G. L., & Parekh, N. (2008). "Skating Down a Steeper Slope: Fear Influences the Perception of Geographical Slant." *Perception*, 37, 321–323.

Stefanucci, J. K., & Storbeck, J. (2009). "Don't Look Down: Emotional Arousal Elevates Height Perception." *Journal of Experimental Psychology: General*, 138, 131–145.

Stein, M. B., & Gorman, J. M. (2001). "Unmasking Social Anxiety Disorder." *Journal of Psychiatry and Neuroscience*, 26(3), 185.

Stonerock, G. L., Hoffman, B. M., Smith, P. J., & Blumenthal, J. A. (2015). "Exercise as Treatment for Anxiety: Systematic Review and Analysis." *Annals of Behavioral Medicine*, 49(4), 542–556.

ten Have, M., de Graaf, R., van Dorsselaer, S., & Beekman, A. (2013). "Lifetime Treatment Contact and Delay in Treatment Seeking after First Onset of a Mental Disorder." *Psychiatric Services*, 64(10), 981–989.

Tolin, D. F., & Foa, E. B. (2006). "Sex Differences in Trauma and Posttraumatic Stress Disorder: A Quantitative Review of 25 Years of Research." *Psychological Bulletin*, 132(6), 959–992.

Vagnoni, E., Lourenco, S. F., & Longo, M. R. (2012). "Threat Modulates Perception of Looming Visual Stimuli." *Current Biology*, 22(19), R826–R827.

van der Watt, G., Laugharne, J., & Janca, A. (2008). "Complementary and Alternative Medicine in the Treatment of Anxiety and Depression." *Current Opinion in Psychiatry*, 21(1), 37–42.

Vasey, M. W., Vilensky, M. R., Heath, J. H., Harbaugh, C. N., Buffington, A. G., & Fazio, R. H. (2012). "It Was as Big as My Head, I Swear! Biased Spider Size Estimation in Spider Phobia." *Journal of Anxiety Disorders*, 26(1), 20–24.

Venkataramana, M., & Pratap, K. V. N. R. (2016). "Effect of Aromatherapy on Dental Patient Anxiety: A Randomized Controlled Trial." *Journal of Indian Association of Public Health Dentistry*, 14(2), 131–134.

Vieweg W. V., Julius D. A., Fernandez A., Beatty-Brooks, M., Hettema, J. M., & Pandurangi, A. K. (2006). "Posttraumatic Stress Disorder: Clinical Features, Pathophysiology, and Treatment." *American Journal of Medicine*, 119, 383.

Vyas, A., Kim, S. K., Giacomini, N., Boothroyd, J. C., & Sapolsky, R. M. (2007). "Behavioral Changes Induced by Toxoplasma Infection of Rodents Are Highly Specific to Aversion of Cat Odors." *Proceedings of the National Academy of Sciences*, 104(15), 6442–6447.

Watkins, L. L., Koch, G. G., Sherwood, A., Blumenthal, J. A., Davidson, J. R. T., O'Connor, C., & Sketch, M. H. (2013). "Association of Anxiety and Depression with All-Cause Mortality in Individuals with Coronary Heart Disease." *Journal of the American Heart Association* 2(2).

Watson, J. B., & Rayner, R. (1920). "Conditioned Emotional Reactions." *Journal of Experimental Psychology*, 3(1), 1.

Weems, C. F., & Costa, N. M. (2005). "Developmental Differences in the Expression of Childhood Anxiety Symptoms and Fears." *Journal of the American Academy of Child and Adolescent Psychiatry*, 44(7), 656–663.

Weinberg, G. H. (1983). *Society and the Healthy Homosexual* (with a new introduction). New York: St. Martin's Press.

Willey, C. R., & Jackson, R. E. (2014). "Visual Field Dependence as a Navigational Strategy." *Attention, Perception & Psychophysics*, 76(4), 1036–1044.

Williams, L. E., & Bargh, J. A. (2008). "Experiencing Physical Warmth Promotes Interpersonal Warmth." *Science*, 322(5901), 606–607. http://doi.org/10.1126/science.1162548.

Williams, M., & Steever, A. (2015). "Cultural Manifestations of Obsessive-Compulsive Disorder." In C. W. Lack (Ed.), *Obsessive-Compulsive Disorders: Etiology, Phenomenology, and Treatment* (pp. 63–83). Fareham, UK: Onus Books.

Wittchen, H.-U., Gloster, A.T., Beesdo-Baum, K., Fava, G.A., & Craske, M.G. (2010). "Agoraphobia: A Review of the Diagnostic Classificatory Position and Criteria." *Depression and Anxiety,* 27(2), 113–133.

Wittchen, H.-U., Nocon, A., Beesdo, K., Pine, D.S., Hofler, M., Lieb, R., & Gloster, A.T. (2008). "Agoraphobia and Panic. Prospective-Longitudinal Relations Suggest a Rethinking of Diagnostic Concepts. *Psychotherapy and Psychosomatics,* 77(3), 147–157.

Wortmann, J.H., Park, C.L., & Edmondson, D. (2011). "Trauma and PTSD Symptoms: Does Spiritual Struggle Mediate the Link?" *Psychological Trauma: Theory, Research, Practice and Policy,* 3(4), 442–452.

Zbozinek, T.D., Rose, R.D., Wolitzky-Taylor, K.B., Sherbourne, C., Sullivan, G., Stein, M.B., . . ., Craske, M.G. (2012). "Diagnostic Overlap of Generalized Anxiety Disorder and Major Depressive Disorder in a Primary Care Sample." *Depression and Anxiety,* 29(12), 1065–1071.

Index

About the Author

Daniel Zwillenberg, PsyD, is a clinical psychologist at McLean Hospital's 3East Intensive DBT Program—a residential program for young women who struggle with self-injury, suicidality, and symptoms of borderline personality disorder (BPD). Dr. Zwillenberg maintains a private practice, where he provides individual therapy and diagnostic evaluations for clients across the age spectrum with a wide range of problems. He is currently interested in developing a treatment protocol that integrates dialectical behavior therapy and exposure and response prevention for patients who have comorbid obsessive-compulsive disorder and BPD. Dr. Zwillenberg also holds an appointment as an instructor in psychology in the Department of Psychiatry at Harvard Medical School.